Parallax

Parallax

Essays on Art, Culture and Technology

DARREN TOFTS

 [AN INTERFACE BOOK]

Distributed in Australia by
Craftsman House,
Tower A, 112 Talavera Road,
North Ryde, Sydney, NSW 2113
Australia

ISBN: 90 5704 007 7
ISSN: 1035 6754

Cover Illustration: Troy Innocent
Design: Jessica Cotterell
Index: John Simkin
Printed by: Kyodo Printing Co., Singapore

For Lucy

Contents

Acknowledgments

I would like to thank the following people for their commitment to the production of this book. Ashley Crawford commissioned this project and has been a fervent supporter ever since. I had the pleasure of working with a number of editors, all of whom made a difficult task more manageable. Ashley Crawford and Sally Van Es edited the manuscript in its early stages, Sarah Bayliss consolidated it and Louise Timko saw it through to completion and was there to the end. Sarah and Louise were also very helpful in securing permissions from various libraries and galleries. Swinburne University of Technology has been very supportive of my work and provided teaching relief and generous financial assistance which covered the reproduction costs for images. I would like to thank Meaghan Morris for her enthusiasm for and generous comments on the book. Hari Ho was most helpful in bringing the whole project together and Rhonda Fitzsimmons, also from Fine Arts Press, offered me tremendous assistance and moral support. Michael Groden put up with my endless questions to do with Joycean copyright matters and made many valuable observations. Thanks to Murray McKeich for helping out with the images. I am grateful to the editors of the following publications for allowing me to reproduce material: Ashley Crawford (*World Art*, *21C*), Bruce James (*Photofile*), Keely Macarow (*Mesh*), Meaghan Morris and Stephen Muecke (*UTS Review*), Barry Weller (*Western Humanities Review*). And finally to Lisa Gye for her love and support.

The essays brought together in *Parallax* have been revised from previously published work or conference presentations: Chapter 1 in *21C*, 1 (1997): pp. 18–21. Chapter 2 in *UTS Review*, 2, 2 (1996): pp. 168–179. Chapter 3 in *Mesh*, 10 (1996): pp. 2–5. Chapter 4 in *Mesh*, 12 (1998/99): pp. 9–13. Chapter 5 is a re-written version of essays published in *World Art*, 1 (1997): pp. 28–33 and *Mesh*, 11 (1997): pp. 13–15. Chapter 6 was originally presented as a paper at the XIVth International James Joyce Symposium, Seville, June 13–18 (1994). Chapter 7 in Editions, 18 (1993): pp. 13–14. Chapter 8 in *Western Humanities Review*, 2, (1995): pp. 159–166. Chapter 9 is an edited version of a paper presented as part of the Centre for Contemporary Photography's Value Added Goods lecture series, Melbourne, 13 November (1996). Chapter 10 in *Photofile*, 53, (1998): pp. 4–7.

Foreword

The various essays brought together in *Parallax* are united by a common theme: that culture at the end of the century needs to be looked at differently. New critical orthodoxies have emerged in the context of an apparent technological transformation of social life in which electronic forms of mediation are replacing familiar habits of interaction associated with physical proximity. Cultural practices have also been transformed. We now talk of digital art, interactive fiction and virtual reality. These practices are frequently discussed as if they have emerged fully-formed from some other dimension and bear no resemblance to the cultural history of this planet. This digital orthodoxy is a kind of cultural amnesia. But it is also a narrow way of looking at the world.

Scanning the cultural landscape of the late twentieth-century, these essays identify uncanny parallels, incongruous juxtapositions and surprising fusions of ideas between the old and the new, the residual and the emergent. Topically diverse, they represent attempts to invent ways of thinking about cultural production as a field of practices that resists homogenization or easy categorization. Cultural criticism is not a pure art. It has more in common, in fact, with T. S. Eliot's industrial portrait of the poetic imagination at work, in which the incongruous and the ill-fitting, such as Spinoza, falling in love, typing and the smell of cabbage cooking, are drawn together into new syntheses under the force of invention. The essay, as a form, has, in many ways, inherited this way of operating, of doing intellectual and imaginative work under conditions in which the eclectic, the inappropriate and the contradictory compete for equal attention in the critical arena.

The sheer breadth of what constitutes cultural production as we approach the new millennium has caused much anxiety among the more traditionally-minded, for whom decorum and the strictures of disciplinary boundaries should continue to be unquestioned qualities of criticism. The complaint that cultural criticism gives as much weight to Donald Duck as William Shakespeare is, of course, nonsense. What has been missed in such grumbling is the simple fact that along with questions of taste and value, the issue of what actually constitutes culture, and for whom, is not a constant quantity.

But there are continuities, as the logic of parallax dictates. Common themes filter through and across the different contexts which give these essays their specific emphases. But at a more general level, contemporary problems to do with representation, expression, authenticity and originality are not exclusive to particular forms of cultural production nor to specific periods. The agon of articulation that we find in those practitioners of the more familiar arts, who endowed the problematics of language with iconic status, underlies cutting-edge discussions of new media, such as digital photography and multimedia. The critical theory marshaled to contour these discussions is itself part of the phenomena it seeks to explain, a series of attitudes to signification, textuality, technology, aesthetics and artifice that recapitulates those artist-theoreticians (Mallarmé, Duchamp, Beckett, Bacon, Cage) who were doing meta-work long before the concept became chic. The ongoing drama over the publication of a correct, authoritative text of James Joyce's *Ulysses*, for instance, is indicative of contemporary anxieties to do with the figure of the author as the centralized matrix of the creative act; an anxiety that resonates in discussions ranging from the work of Jeff Koons to digital photography. Cultural practices such as sampling, quotation and collagic-reassemblage, supported by wilful (mis)applications of deconstructive poetics, have re-defined the author's role as a kind of director of found materials, a ventriloquist of the already said. Far from being monumental, *Ulysses* has become something of a discursive formation in its own right, and the diverse practices of post-poetics are, arguably, locutions constituted within this formation. In this respect, then, one of the themes of *Parallax* concerns the perception that art-works once exclusively associated with a now historical modernity, such as *Ulysses*, continue to exert a profound influence on contemporary understandings of culture.

Alongside the usual suspects of media theory, Joyce is essential reading for anyone wanting to come to terms with important debates about the obsolescence of the book and the emergence of an electronic, post-literate culture. But so too are other figures and concepts discussed in this book. There is no question that we live in an age in which very few features of social and cultural life have not been touched by technology. But the contemporary preoccupation with technology as being in some profound way *a la mode* is insidiously deceptive. It would be a waste of time to argue that we have always had technology. However, the wrong kinds of questions are continuously asked about the relationship between residual technological forms and the kinds of technological developments that have led to the formation of cyberculture. Discussions of "dead media" abound in cyber discourse, usually cheek by jowl with panegyrics to "new media." But beyond the narrowness of the chronological approach, there are other ways of looking at the way media interrelate. In what ways do hypermedia practices have to be reconciled with those media, such as the book, cinema, television, animation, etc., which have contributed to its recombinant logic? Where are we to locate emergent art forms based on hypermedia, such as the virtual reality environment? Is the museum or the gallery an appropriate space for this work and if not, what kinds of aesthetic questions need to be looked at to determine such a space? The work of Australian artists Troy Innocent and Jon McCormack has been significant for not only dramatizing some of the possibilities of an emergent digital aesthetic, but for also generating serious and sustained discussion of the institutional and architectural questions prompted by such art.

In the search for novelty, theorists of new media desiderate endlessly about non-linearity, interactivity and all manner of non-hierarchical, liberatory practices. Changing the angle of perception slightly, to include history in the pantheon of hypermedia, rather than exclude it, we can start to see things differently. Rather than being new of necessity, hypermedia's contribution to and advancement of the cultural apparatus of representation lies in its re-constitution of the historical practices it re-combines. Interactivity didn't come into being with multimedia games, virtual reality environments or electronic mail. Interactivity, as a phenomenon of electronic media, has modified, rather than revolutionized, the symbiotic relationship between art-work and consumer that any communications medium or aesthetic experience necessitates. It has given added emphasis to those modes of engagement which, historically, have required a more active participation on behalf of audiences, spectators and readers. When the proponents of hypertext discourse upon the anarchism of interactive fiction, they would do well to remember the kind of "user" Marcel Duchamp was trying to invent with his manifold assemblage of the *Large Glass* and *Green Box*. Here was a truly dramatic cultural practice, in which the interactions of every individual were not optional or collateral, but absolutely vital to the creation of the artwork.

These essays are, above all, concerned with exploring interferences to normative perceptions of language, technology, creativity and reception. These interferences are suggestive of multifarious experimental practices that have yet to be fully absorbed and digested by the voracious mechanisms of cultural change. Cultural practices emerge, in part, from appropriating and domesticating the once bold and threatening. Just think of cubism's co-optation as design and of the relegation of abstraction to a signature style for be-bop, hep-catness and all manner of off-the-wall-ness. But certain inflections, attitudes and energies, for which we still, perhaps, don't have a nomenclature, persist and find expression in a new apparatus. In the age of cyberculture and hypermedia, then, there is still much to be learned from artists and art practices that don't seem to fit in, or belong to, the *fin de siècle* age of electronic technology.

Darren Tofts, Melbourne, 1999.

[1] Machine Metaphysics

Ever since Donna Haraway published her landmark 1985 essay "Manifesto for Cyborgs,"[1] cultural critics have been besotted with cybernetic organisms. More metaphor than machine, Haraway's cyborg serves as a potent talisman for the global convergence of human body with electronic network, extending our post-Futurist romance with mechanical technology. However, in an age that has seen Norbert Wiener replace Sigmund Freud as the arbiter of the psyche, human interface technology is prompting some significant re-thinking of ancient questions concerning the nature of being. Cybernetics, ostensibly the science of self-regulating systems, was, like psychoanalysis, fundamentally a study of human behavior. The basic idea was that the study of mechanical processes of response and feedback could be seen as analogies of organic behavior. Accordingly, mechanical malfunctions could provide valid insights into dysfunctional symptoms (such as neuroses). However, the cybernetic gaze can also be inverted in such a way that attention to ourselves can provide critical insight into the behavior of machines. Instead of the cyberphiliac yearning to transcend the meat and become more like a machine, à la Kroker, the development of artificial intelligence and robotics, à la Moravec, forces us to consider a potentially frightening scenario: what if our machines can become human?

The cybernetic organism is more human than machine. It is the Promethean dream revisited, the human body augmented and improved by technology: anyone with a hearing-aid or a heart pacemaker can proudly stand cheek by mechanical jowl with Stelarc and proudly claim the appellation as their own. Haraway's catchcry "We are cyborgs" attests as much as anything else to this recombinant ethic, the will to defy the obsolescence of the flesh. However, the gradual domestication of the idea of the cyborg as a technologically improved human has had the effect of obscuring from view that other borderline creature that melds human flesh and electronic circuitry, the android. The android, or humanoid robot, is definitely more machine than human. While it doesn't (yet) exist outside of science fiction, and has virtually been debased as a misunderstood synonym for cyborg, the android is actually more suggestive of the metaphysical problems that arise when we start to think of machines in human terms, and blur philosophical distinctions between human and machine.

Just as the cyborg has had an undeniable sociological and anthropological impact on cultural criticism, the android has also figured within popular culture as a kind of control that facilitates insight into what it means to be human. The shapely beauty Will Robinson falls in love with in *Lost in Space*, the innumerable constructs that "people" the works of Philip K. Dick, or Data on *Star Trek: The Next Generation*, all provide a context of Otherness that enables the quark, strangeness and charm of *humanitas* to be cast in proud relief. Of these examples Dick is, not surprisingly, the most hostile to the idea of the android, simply because it *is* artificial, something that masquerades as a human. It is this element of deception, of "fierce cold things ... trying to pass themselves off as human but are not," that Dick betrays again and again in his writing. The fact that these simulacra (the term Dick most frequently used to describe androids) are designed to deceive, to make humans think that they are human also, suggests that the ontology of the android, the nature of its being, was effectively bound up with how it appears to others. Reflecting on this in a 1976 essay called "Man, Android, and Machine," Dick concluded, remarkably, that the difference between a human and an android was not a difference of essence (as we would reasonably expect), but rather of behavior.

This astonishing notion flies in the face of most of our philosophical and anthropological verities. We like to believe that our behavior reliably reflects our essence, that the seemliness of things bears a direct correlation to a fixed reality. However, the nature of an android is such that we have no way of knowing that its behavior *does not* reflect its essence. In Dick's stories, for instance, androids simulate human behavior so well that real people don't know that they are not human. In *Do Androids Dream of Electric Sheep?* this problem is so acute that the burden of authenticity, of having to prove that you are in fact human, falls virtually on everyone. Similarly, humans are gripped with self-doubt and paranoia in the fear that they may in fact be androids. In the presence of androids, then, ambivalence and existential dread characterize any attempt to reliably locate the true nature of being. Everything begins and ends with appearances, surfaces without depth, copied human behavior lacking a basis in human nature. In this respect, the android *queers* the distinct categories of human and machine. The term queer has been used politically in recent years to designate same-sex desire, without declaring which sex is doing the desiring, and which is the object of desire. Similarly, the behavior of an android foregrounds the human without having to declare its essential difference from it (it is essentially inhuman). Like the simulacrum in Dick's novel *We Can Build You* sent in to a pizza shop by its manufacturer as a demonstration of this very issue: "You'll see how convincing this simulacrum is ... when it orders its own pizza." Its behavior, then, queers any notional distinction between its appearance and its essence. This is a big problem for metaphysics (as Dick was quick to recognize), for on the basis of how human an android appears to be, there can no longer be any claim to an essential humanness against which, and in relation to which, androids are the Other.

If the cyborg represents the outer reaches of the evolutionary dream of the human body improved by technology, the android is the nightmarish flip-side of that dream, a figure of queerness that collapses reliable, normative ontologies such as human and machine. In this respect, the character of Data is much more user-friendly (and certainly more straight) than Dick's Rachael Rosen (from *Do Androids Dream of Electric Sheep?*). He is in no doubt that he is an android and is forever trying to understand and appropriate behavior that he knows is decidedly human (humor, though, is something totally "alien" to him). Rachael, like many of the other hapless chimaera of Dick's border worlds, doesn't know she is an artificial construct, until it is revealed to her by the bounty hunter Rick Deckard. In a cathartic moment, Rachael is confronted with a peculiarly human situation, the metaphysical conundrum. Having failed the Voigt-Kampff test (Deckard's only means of identifying an android), Rachael is forced to consider what it means to know that she is not actually alive, that she doesn't have a human nature. Rachael has been programmed to forget that she is an android, implanted with false memories of a childhood that she never experienced, an identity that she doesn't possess. At this moment she inhabits a metaphysical utopia in the literal sense of the term: a nowhere.

We are familiar from speculative fiction and particular genres of postmodern writing with the troubling, ontological disquiet caused by the intrusion of the unreal or the fabulatory into the domain of the feasible. Rachael's "self" revelation, however, is a curious instance of the contamination of the unreal by the real, the inhuman by the human, since a concern with self is a decidedly human trait. Machines, such as computers, can be infected by viruses that corrupt binary relationships between ones and zeros. What, though, of the ghost in the machine? What if androids were to be contaminated by a meme, a metaphysical virus that invaded and colonized the host, thereby altering not its arrangement of data, but its ontological equilibrium? Imagine the consequences of an android that no longer simulated human behaviour, but actually *became* more human, of artificial human life mutating into human life. In this respect the machine could be thought of as a kind of revenant, coming into life from a state of unlife. Under such conditions androids would without a doubt dream of electric sheep, soft watches, and red kings to boot. As fanciful as such an idea might be, the idea that an android could acquire a metaphysics through viral contamination is a tantalizing abstraction that promises to counteract cyberculture's obsession with bodies, as well as the evangelical desire to see the organic body function with the infallible monotony of a machine. While we want to be more like them, they may become more like us.

One particular episode of *Star Trek: The Next Generation* featured a holographic battle of wits between Sherlock Holmes (Data) and his nemesis Moriarty (an avatar configured by the Holodeck computer program). During the course of the simulation, Moriarty develops agency and human consciousness, the result of an ontological confusion in the instructions given to the computer to find a worthy adversary for Data (a "real" entity), rather than Holmes, the fictional character played by Data (a confusion worthy of Pirandello or the author of *Slaughterhouse-Five*, Kilgore Trout). This was in itself a beautiful irony, since Data didn't have a self to begin with (he isn't even technically alive), yet the Holodeck had interpreted that he must have one given that Holmes was his fictional alter ego. This ontological slippage enables Moriarty to motivate real actions with real effects, to think for himself and thereby become a genuine threat to others. In other words, he stepped momentarily out of virtual reality into actuality as a human being. He is, of course, eventually defeated, for even science fiction can't tolerate the idea of machine metaphysics. Moriarty's defeat is tinged with *Star Trek*'s trademark nostalgia for the human, but with a difference. As he shuffles off the holographic stage, he faces the death-like predicament of being stored as so much random access memory. This can obviously be read as a parody of the will to virtuality, the human desire for digital immersion. But, more profoundly, it is a freeze-frame of the no-man's-land of border metaphysics, of machines becoming human and turning into machines again, and somehow being aware that the implications of this bizarre, elegiac transubstantiation do make a difference.

1 "Manifesto for Cyborgs" was originally published in *Socialist Review*, 80, 1985. It was later revised as a chapter in Haraway's *Simians, Cyborgs, and Women: The Reinvention of Nature* (London: Routledge, 1991).

[2] Hyperlogic, the Avant-garde and Other Intransitive Acts

Lautréamont fixed the concept of Surrealism for future generations in a now famous, formulated phrase: the "chance encounter, on an operating table, of a sewing machine and an umbrella." The phrase has come to identify the movement as a metonymy of strangeness. However, Lautréamont was anticipating much more than an artistic movement. He was describing a mode of thought. But it was not just any mode of thought. It was an alternative logic; a way of making a different kind of sense of the world. Nor was it that new. Examples of it can be found in the macaronic poets of the twelfth century, the "metaphysical" wit epitomized in the work of Donne and Marvell, and in the Symbolist poetry of Mallarmé, Rimbaud and Valéry. Critical discourse, too, has monitored outbreaks of this logic, though it has not always valued it. Samuel Johnson recognised it in Shakespeare and Sterne, and was quick to censure, writing the former's equivocations off as diversionary quibbles, the latter's paratactics as temporary idiosyncracy.[1] Although the work of F. R. Leavis has all but disappeared from critical discourse these days, he was in fact remarkable as a champion of this tradition of intellectual conception which, to make a link from Leavis to T. S. Eliot, "is constantly amalgamating disparate experience," such as falling in love, reading Spinoza, the noise of a typewriter and the smell of cooking; all while etherised upon an operating table.[2] Since 1938, when Johan Huizinga published his *Homo Ludens*, we have described this tendency as "ludic." Deleuze and Guattari called it rhizomorphic. To Leavis and Eliot it was simply a matter of poetic sensibility. In describing this sensibility as a machine "which could devour any kind of experience,"[3] Eliot looked forward to hypermedia, and anticipated the most recent manifestation of this mode of thought.

Eliot looked forward. In my genealogy he did, at any rate. But this is no ordinary genealogy. This is the kind of genealogy that finds traces through association. Like *Lipstick Traces*. Associations, as Laurence Sterne knew only too well, get you off the point. But in the process they open up new ideas, new paths that didn't seem to be there before. Paths that make a better mystery out of history. Gilbert Rodman wrote that in an article on historiography, drawing on Deleuze and Guattari and rhizomorphic writing.[4] Eliot, Marcus, Sterne, Rodman, Deleuze, Guattari. Before I wrote this paragraph I had no conscious intention of linking these authors together. Francis Bacon once commented that he created images that the conscious mind would never make. Better add Bacon to the list.

What is happening here is a form of extended thinking, rather like those famous conceits of Donne. There it is again. Extended thinking, extended metaphor. (*Aside, future perfect*. The problem with writing is that the improvised nature of my composition of this piece will always be experienced *a posteriori* by whoever chooses to read it. The formation of the "previous" link has already passed, and what was impromptu for me has taken on the look of predictability for my reader. What was invention is now convention, a premise already radiating the look of decidability, familiarity. Attempting to perform hyperlogic in an essay is a risky business in the first place, for the creation, as opposed to re-iteration of ideas, has never been part of the spectacle of the form. In terms of its very conventions, it is a form which projects outcomes, not processes. Hyperlogic is a "heuretic"[5] procedure that invents a map of ideation. How to avoid a simple re-tracing of the map, at the expense of the logic of invention, is the question). The conceit embodies a lateral form of reasoning, which starts from a surprising, perhaps accidental perception of relation (coitus likened to a flea bite, for instance) and follows through all its possible implications within the context of association. It's the kind of speculative, creative risk-taking that C.S.Peirce described as abductive reasoning, and that Jorge Luis Borges admired in Paul Valéry's writing: "'Idea for a frightening story: it is discovered that the only remedy for cancer is living human flesh. Consequences."[6] In the Surrealist cinema of Dalí and Buñuel this extended mode of thought found its expression as a "dizzying, revelatory version of psychoanalytic free association," what Adrian Martin has called hyperlogic.[7]

Tristram Shandy. "The Garden of Forking Paths." *A Thousand Plateaus*. I keep coming across these texts in discussions of hypermedia. Commentators on new media are increasingly attracted to their indeterminacy, their capacity for or articulation of different pathways, multiple narrative choice, like in *The Phantom of Liberty*. I was always fascinated by the indifference of the camera in that film, its promiscuity (in the literal meaning of the term) and the ease with which it was distracted from one narrative by the unexpected possibility of others, sprouting off like so many aerials, linked by the appearance of a character or an event. No story was ever finished, everything was

John Cage preparing a piano, early 1960s, photograph by Ross Welser. Courtesy the John Cage Trust, New York.

indefinite. Duchamp's work was indefinite. His *Large Glass* was never completed, was never complete. He described it as "definitively unfinished."[8] The same can be said of *Ulysses*; Joyce didn't achieve textual closure, he simply stopped writing. Neither Duchamp nor Joyce was prepared to complete the creative act; both desired to sustain it. Cage prepared the piano. He modified it in ways that enabled the production of unexpected sounds, sounds the instrument was not designed to make. Sounds over which he had no control.

Before this gets too far advanced let's just pause for a minute. This kind of free association is highly charged. It's no wonder Tristan Tzara and William Butler Yeats were so turned on to it. Once you get into a rhythm it's hard to stop, and as a mode of composition it's highly productive. The work seems to just run away from you, to take on a life of its own. Bacon notes this again and again in his dialogues with David Sylvester. Hang on. Alright, I will allow myself one further dalliance with the Bacon reference to clinch the point I'm trying to make:

David Sylvester: What about luck in your work?

Francis Bacon: I think that accident, which I would call luck, is one of the most important and fertile aspects of it, because, if anything works for me, I feel it is nothing I have made myself, but something which chance has been able to give me. But it's true to say that over a great many years I have been thinking about chance and about the possibilities of using what chance can give, and I never know how much it is pure chance and how much it is manipulation of it.

David Sylvester: You probably find that you can get better at manipulating it.

Francis Bacon: One possibly gets better at manipulating the marks that have been made by chance, which are the marks that one made quite outside reason. As one conditions oneself by time and by working to what happens, one becomes more alive to what the accident has proposed for one.[9]

Bacon, like Samuel Beckett, was interested in that intersection between chance and choice in the creative process. Accident offers you something unexpected which you can then work with and develop wilfully. Invention, in this sense, becomes a form of augmentation, a kind of assisted readymade. You stumble upon the snowshovel, but what are you going to do with it? Chance presents you with an entryway, an *aperçu*. Perhaps that's how Marcus felt when he first heard the *Sex Pistols*: "It was there from the start— a possibility, one of the alleys leading off the free street."[10] What has chance offered me in the previous train of thought?

Three enticing names draw my attention, like a kind of punctum. Duchamp, Joyce, Cage. Establish a contextual lattice: easy, their most infamous signatures. *The Large Glass*. Duchamp described *The Large Glass* as a "catalogue of ideas," to be looked at and thought about from "all associative angles."[11] His method of generating this process was interactive, an exploitation of indeterminacy. *The Green Box* which accompanied *The Large Glass* contained 93 prompts, potential links capable of generating chain reactions of ideas. Rather like an avant-garde lucky dip, the random selection of any of his notes meant that the ways of looking at the *Glass* were unpredictable and unrepeatable, since there was no pre-determined or official way of combining the notes with the *Glass*. Cage, too, envisaged that no two experiences of any of his works would be the same. He was very much attracted to the Duchampian notion of "indecisive reunion"[12] as a means of conceiving the interface between spectator and spectacle. He required his audience to be "omni-attentive,"[13] to listen to everything at once. His *4'33": Tacet for any instruments* liberates sound "for an infinite play of interpretation."[14] Anything may happen. Anything does happen, and the audience is free to make choices about which sounds they want to listen to and reflect on. Listening in Cage, like contemplation in Duchamp, is conjunctural: "... the bringing of things together that wouldn't be together unless you brought them together."[15] You are always already in *The Large Glass*, since it is impossible to look *at it*. There can only ever be an interface. Cage's audience, too, is not outside the performance, but part of it, ambient like sound itself. In *Finnegans Wake*, too, there is no beginning, no middle, no end. There is only the state of being inter, in between, in the midst of things: "A way a lone a last a loved a long the riverrun." In the *Wake* Joyce created a "proteiform graph," a "polyhedron of scripture."[16] His "piously forged palimpsest" (182) is the ideal book yearned for by Deleuze, the virtual page on which all writing and all history exist at one and the same time: "In the buginning is the woid." (378) You never read the *Wake*, you play it, following the splintering of words as they metamorphose within themselves, and at the same time flow throughout this "allaphbed," (18) filtering sedimentary echoes and resonances along the riverrun. Reading time will have to be

MARCEL DUCHAMP, The Large Glass, 1915–23.
Philadelphia Museum of Art:
Bequest of Katherine S. Dreier.
Reproduced with permission.

extended in this library of babel. You may need to cultivate an "ideal insomnia." (120) Or, better still, augment your intelligence.

A common thread starts to take shape: Duchamp, Cage and Joyce all created instances into which someone could intervene to make choices and judgements that they were not willing to make. Myron Krueger has written something very similar about hypertext. In fact I think I've pretty well paraphrased him from memory.[17] All three actively promoted chance discovery over any notion of authorial pre-determination. Duchamp's celebrated indifference is their signature, their invitation to interactivity: come into this work, feel free to go anywhere you like, do anything you like, whenever you like.

Interface, indeterminacy, interactivity. These are the principle characteristics of hypermedia. Hypermedia such as the Internet and hypertext reputedly offer us a powerful form of intelligence augmentation, a kind of electronic thought. The alinear pathways made possible by URL jumping on the Internet (you can jump to any point from any point, without having to go back to the beginning) have much in common with the paratactics of Buñuel and Joyce, the aleatory poetics of Cage and Duchamp. The same can be said of the negotiation of virtual documents such as hypertexts. My first experience of a multimedia encyclopaedia began with a beautiful, high resolution image of an African village. This was quickly left behind as I pursued a series of links within links which transported me from plate-tectonics to Geosyncline theory to the Devonian period. What began as a discrete image became a "docuverse." While this kind of extended logic can be harnessed for research purposes, its mechanism actually promotes purposelessness. This is the nature of a virtual document, in that your attention to the immediate material in front of you is always being distracted elsewhere by highlighted links; you are always being prompted to go somewhere else, to a parallel, linked document. Apart, then, from their contribution to the advancement of media and communications technologies, hypermedia should be considered as an extension of the modernist avant-garde.[18]

The idea of activity without an ostensible point, other than the performing of the act itself, was central in Cage, Duchamp and Joyce. Cage often talked about "purposeful purposelessness."[19] For him it was part of his fascination with Zen notions of contemplation, of intense attention to the here and now; an excentrifugal force of static activity. Activity that doesn't go anywhere, but simply is. Duchamp's notorious indifference was in fact a wilful relinquishing of authority, as well as an attempt to encourage a conceptual, rather than retinal engagement with his work. Joyce was perhaps the most uncompromising of the three in this respect, demanding of readers of *Ulysses* and

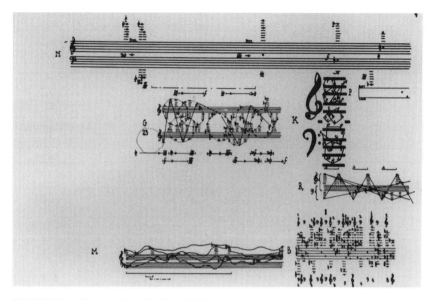

JOHN CAGE, Solo for Piano from Concert for Piano and Orchestra, 1957–58, page 9. Copyright 1960 by Henmar Press Inc./ C. F. Peters Corporation. Reproduced with permission.

Finnegans Wake that they devote as much (if not more) time to the activity of reading these texts as to life itself. This is perhaps one of the few instances in Joyce where we should treat suspected irony as being dead straight. Joyce, as we know, was highly superstitious, and blamed the commencement of the Second World War on some kind of conspiracy, aimed at distracting the literate world from the world of his invention. This was no bravado. He really believed it.

Hugh Kenner once described Swift and Sterne as a "pair of tutelary deities," so frequently do they appear throughout the *Wake*.[20] My tutelary trinity have thrown up some useful insights into contemporary hypermedia culture, especially in terms of our perceptions of the links between artistic or recreational activity, time and communication. Hypermedia imply an especially conative form of engagement. Purposelessness and pleasure, in this respect, acquire a special meaning as play. Towards the end of *Virtual Reality*, Howard Rheingold observes that while the concept of play "is fraught with taboos in our culture," it is nonetheless central to creativity and invention. When "aimless play" is balanced with "focused, directed activity" (a good description of the human/computer interface), it enables us to learn to think in new ways.[21] As part of the fabric of the every day, in an emergent cybernetic culture, the much publicized presence of hypermedia as a recreational form, attests to the way in which *divertisse-*

ment has always been at home in popular culture. Perhaps this unfortunate recognition of the high/low culture cliché partly explains the charges of unintelligibility made against Duchamp, Joyce and Cage; audiences were still approaching them as though they were purveyors of high art. Duchamp's readymade aesthetic, Joyce's "scrupulous meanness" and Cage's beatification of noise should have alerted the cautious to their love of the contingent here and now. Dada and Surrealism, it should be remembered, began life with the detritus of the streets, the flea markets and the paraphernalia of the every day, such as *Le Figaro*, sewing machines, umbrellas, etc. The culture of every day life in the age of cybernetics is certainly becoming more sedentary, and more housebound as well. Just think of "Microsoft Home."

The short history of the Internet has already revealed a considerable level of addiction. The medium has been avidly pursued as an end in itself, despite whatever one finds "of use" to download. Its principle metaphor of surfing is suggestive of its dynamism and its hedonism (though not all critics are so convinced of its aptness).[22] The emergent culture of interactive fiction is no different. Take the case of the San Francisco lawyer who was so consumed by the activity of playing *Myst* that, in a situation resembling a Borges story, the virtual experience began to infiltrate "real" life: "The only problem was when I began clicking on things in real life. I'd see a manhole cover and think, 'Hmmm, that looks pretty interesting,' and my forefinger would start to twitch.'"[23] Interactive multi-media is shaping up as the successor of cinema, television and video as the twentieth century's latest "all-consuming consumption," to use Philip Brophy's resonant phrase.[24] When the derogatory connotations are shed from the notion of purposeless activity it starts to look very much like popular culture, by any other name.

One of the advantages of this kind of historiography, as Greil Marcus has demonstrated, is the formation of alternative histories, generated according to principles of serendipity, audacious comparisons and unexpected links:

... late in 1976 a record called "Anarchy in the U.K." was issued in London, and this event launched a transformation of pop music all over the world. Made by a four-man rock 'n' roll band called the Sex Pistols, and written by singer Johnny Rotten, the song distilled, in crudely poetic form, a critique of modern society once set out by a small group of Paris-based intellectuals. First organized in 1952 as the Lettrist International, and refounded in 1957 at a conference of European avant-garde artists as the Situationist International, the group gained its greatest notoriety during the French revolt of May 1968, when the premises of its critique were distilled into crudely poetic slogans and spray-painted across the walls of Paris, after which the critique was given up to history and the group disappeared. The group looked back to the surrealists of the 1920s, the dadaists who made their names during and just after the First World War, the young Karl Marx, Saint-Just, various medieval heretics, and the Knights of the Round Table.[25]

John Lydon. John of Leyden (Johan Huizinga was rector of Leyden University.)

Alternative histories are interesting in that they provide another way of conceiving a particular terrain, in the process uncovering the assumptions that underlie "official" histories. In terms of my immediate interest, the history of hyperlogic, and by extension hypermedia, the official history has already been written, in books such as Howard Rheingold's *Virtual Reality*. Duchamp, Joyce and Cage don't figure in Rheingold's scheme of things. He works with a different trinity: Vannevar Bush, Douglas Englebart, and Ivan Sutherland, men whose backgrounds were in computer science rather than the avant-garde arts. Not to mention the formative context of the military-industrial complex. However in "mystory" Duchamp, Joyce and Cage are more relevant to my understanding of hypermedia and its associated logic. I'm drawing here, of course, on the concept of mystory theorized by Greg Ulmer in *Teletheory. Grammatology in the Age of Video*, and put into practice (to construct his own hypermedia mystory) in *Heuretics. The Logic of Invention*. As with McKenzie Wark's notion of "vectoral writing" in *Virtual Geography. Living With Global Media Events*,(26) I am mindful that one doesn't begin to write mystorically, since one is already in mystorical mode. Mystory has no official beginning, as in traditional historiography, since the place of its conception, its place of growth is the matrix of discursive crossroads that constitutes my own cultural archive.

This concept of being situated within a designated subjectivity is central to Ulmer's conception of mystory. It is context sensitive. The contemporary imperative to be all-inclusive (mystory, history, herstory, theirstory) diminishes as a default position in the formation of mystory, for the simple reason that it fulfills the politically correct urge to let specified subjectivities speak in the full context of their locality. As an academic trained in the English department of the early 1980s, it is predictable and appropriate for me to draw on so-called canonical writers as a frame of reference. The canonical, though, is hardly a default standard against which the avant-garde is to be measured, for during those formative years English was beset by the specter of critical theory. As a result, the canon has always been something conjunctural rather than essential for me, something always in relation to adversarial forms of theory and practice, something caught up within a process of implicit problematization. The work of Leavis and

Eliot is certainly there to be drawn on, but it is inextricably bound up with the insurgence of theory as a synchronous archive. It is not so much a matter of reviving Leavis and Eliot in the context of hypermedia, but of their unavoidable association in the matrix of relations constituted by Darren Tofts' speculation of a possible historiography of hyperlogic. In this respect it is perhaps more appropriate to invoke Ulmer's notion of "chorography," a term derived from Plato's "chora," meaning space, or place of growth. In Ulmer's grammatology, the chora is highly idiosyncratic, the equivalent of Derrida's signature effect. The chorographic event also known as *Heuretics* makes this clear, marking its performance with the scriptural equivalent of Ulmer DNA, the relief map of his conceptual imprint:

> I am developing an analogy for chorography, saying that electronic writing is like performing a tableau vivant from Beau Geste as part of a follies show at a frontier saloon commemorating the Columbus quincentenary. Once I had the idea for the scene to use as the basis for the tableau — Beau's "Viking Funeral" at Fort Zinderneuf — I still had to learn how to act the part. I decided to try Method acting.[27]

In a similar way, think of this essay as a kind of compilation tape, made up of songs that have meaning and resonance for me within the context of a specific act of speculation. It is not only the eclectic selection of tunes, but the relations between them, their contiguity, that suggests the signature event. It is at this moment that cultural studies becomes vectoral, genuinely engaged with the multiple relations and relational multiplicities of the every day. I could approach this topic "tomorrow" and produce a totally different chorographic event. I am always *in medias res*.

The idea of immersion in textuality is very much in critical vogue at the moment. Immersion is also the orienting grand narrative of hypermedia, especially virtual, or artificial reality environments. The recognition of this fact, though, prompts a more fundamental consideration of what is happening to our assumptions about language as communication. Are the Internet and hypertext forms of communication? I think not. Why not? Perhaps we can learn something from poststructuralism's encounter with the *Wake*.

Poststructuralist theory, especially in its reflexive play, is an engagement with the purposeless activity of textuality, with "la dissémination de la texture." It's in no way surprising that critics have made it *de rigueur* to comment on the parallels between hypermedia and poststructuralism, especially when so many of the key words associated with new media formations echo the much maligned patois of Derrida and company.[28] As Gregory Ulmer has suggested, several influential commentators have observed that hypermedia "literalizes" or repre-sents the material embodiment of poststructuralist (mostly French) theories of text. Many of the most controversial notions of textualism expressed by recent French critics (for example, the death of the author or the decentering of meaning), notions that seemed bizarre in the context of the book apparatus, are literal qualities of hyper-media.[29]

Similar parallels between *différance* and Joyce's language in the *Wake* have been noted. Indeed, Joyce's·writing, like Beckett's, became a kind of proving ground for poststructuralist theories in the 1960s and 1970s. Part of this process involved an exploration into the dynamics of resistance to, and denial of Joyce's use of language in the *Wake*. Stephen Heath, for example, drew attention to the historical stigmatization of the *Wake* in terms of "the impossibility of converting that text into a critical object" and the subsequent reduction of its writing "to the simple carrier of a message (a meaning) that it will be the critic's task to 'extract from its enigmatic envelope.'"[30] In other words, Heath argued that the critical treatment of the *Wake* as an "aberration" was based on the assumption of language as a transitive form of communication. The idea of language as a vehicle, a mover of a meaning from a here to a there, was clearly a nonsense in the *Wake*, since it develops "according to a fundamental incompletion; the text produces a derisive hesitation of sense, the final revelation of meaning being always for 'later.'" (31) Heath argued that the language of the *Wake* disarmed ("decon-struct" was just coming into vogue) extant practices of criticism that were predicated on the assumption of transitivity. "Where criticism *ex*plicates, opening out the folds of the writing in order to arrive at the meaning, *Finnegans Wake* is offered as a perma-nent *inter*plication, a work of folding and unfolding in which every element becomes always the fold of another in a series that knows no point of rest." (32) That is, lan-guage in the *Wake* is intransitive; it does not lead to a point outside the materiality of its own play. And that was its problem. It was an accelerated instance of the funda-mental problem of literariness theorized by the Formalists; literary discourse trans-forms and violates "ordinary" language. Our problems begin when we think we can read the former as if it were the latter.

This is the fascination and, for many, the problem with hypermedia. They are intran-sitive. They constitute an emergent signifying activity that does not take an object, and in this sense, are not communicational. It's one thing to have to recognize intransi-tivity in the experimental arts, but they are, after all is said and done, where transgres-sion is played out. It is another thing, though, to have to recognize it in media that are increasingly becoming part of the fabric of the every day. I would not want to make the claim, though, that Net surfing or interactive gameplaying are equivalent, intransitive activities to reading *Finnegans Wake*. Far from it, in fact. Hypermedia have a lot of catching up to do. Jacques Derrida made the claim nearly twenty years ago that computer technology was a *"bricolage* of a prehistoric child's toys" compared to *Ulysses* and *Finnegans Wake*.[31] It is just as valid a claim today. However, they are alike in as much as they privilege the processes of doing, of gameplay, of activity over the *im*mediate yielding up of meaning. Appropriating Heath, Net surfers and interactive gameplayers no longer seek to master textuality, but accede to the play of incompletion, they agree "to become its actor." (32)

The issues generated by mystory of hypermedia, and their consequences for the ongoing manifestation of hyperlogic and the avant-garde, will have to be ...

1 Samuel Johnson, "Preface to *The Plays of William Shakespeare,*" in *Samuel Johnson. Selected Poetry and Prose*, ed. by Frank Brady and W.K.Wimsatt (Berkeley: University of California Press, 1977) p. 309; quoted in James Boswell, *Life of Johnson* (Oxford: Oxford University Press, 1980), p. 696.

2 T.S. Eliot: *Selected Essays* (London: Faber & Faber, 1976), p. 287.

3 Eliot, p. 287.

4 Gilbert Rodman, "Making a better mystery out of history," *Meanjin*, 52, 2 (1993) pp. 295–312.

5 For an understanding of the term "heuretic" as I am using it here, see D.Tofts, R.Kinnane & A.Haig, "I Owe the Discovery of this Image to the Convergence of a Student and A Photocopier," *Southern Review,* "Teaching the Postmodern" Special Number, 27, 3 (1994) p. 257.

6 Quoted in Jorge-Luis Borges, *Labyrinths*, ed. by Donald A. Yates & James E. Irby (Harmondsworth: Penguin, 1976), p. 11.

7 Adrian Martin, "The Artificial Night: Surrealism and Cinema," in *Surrealism. Revolution by Night* (Canberra: National Gallery of Australia Publications, 1993) p. 194.

8 Quoted in *Marcel Duchamp*, ed. Pontus Hulten (London: Thames & Hudson, 1993) unpaginated.

9 David Sylvester, *The Brutality of Fact. Interviews with Francis Bacon*, 3rd edn (London: Thames & Hudson, 1990) pp. 52–3.

10 Greil Marcus, *Lipstick Traces. A Secret History of the Twentieth Century* (London: Secker & Warburg, 1989) p. 10.

11 Marcel Duchamp, quoted in Hulten.

12 Marcel Duchamp, "Kind of Sub-Title. Delay in Glass," in *The Bride Stripped Bare by Her Bachelors, Even. A Typographic Version*, by Richard Hamilton, trans. by George Heard Hamilton (Stuttgart: Edition Hansjörg Mayer, 1976) p. i.

13 John Cage, quoted in *John Cage*, ed. Richard Kostelanetz (London: Allen Lane, 1971) p. 167.

14 John Cage, *Silence* (London, Marion Boyars, 1987) p. 59.

15 John Cage, quoted in *Cage, Cunningham & Johns, Dancers on a Plane* (London, Thames & Hudson, 1989) p. 52.

16 James Joyce, *Finnegans Wake* (London: Faber & Faber, 1975) p. 107. Further references to this edition are given after quotations in the text.

17 Myron Krueger, in Michael Heim, *The Metaphysics of Virtual Reality* (New York: Oxford University

Press, 1993) viii.

18 See Nicholas Zurbrugg, *The Parameters of Postmodernism* (London: Routledge, 1994) p. 133 and Jay David Bolter, *Writing Space. The Computer, Hypertext and the History of Writing* (Hillsdale: Erlbaum, 1991) p. 132.

19 John Cage, *Indeterminacy. New Aspect of Form in Instrumental and Electronic Music*, Soundrecording (Folkways FT 3704, 1958).

20 Hugh Kenner, *The Stoic Comedians. Flaubert, Joyce and Beckett* (Berkeley: University of California Press, 1974) p. 48.

21 Howard Rheingold, *Virtual Reality* (London: Secker & Warburg, 1991) p. 372.

22 Lisa Gye, "Surfing the Internet," *Metro*, 101 (1995) pp. 83–4.

23 John Carroll, "Guerrillas in the *Myst*," *Wired*, August (1994), pp. 70–3.

24 Philip Brophy, "Program Notes," *Trash and Junk Culture Exhibition*, Australian Centre for Contemporary Art, Melbourne, March, 1989, unpaginated.

25 Greil Marcus, p. 18.

26 McKenzie Wark, *Virtual Geography. Living With Global Media Events* (Bloomington: Indiana University Press, 1994).

27 Gregory Ulmer, *Heuretics. The Logic of Invention* (Baltimore: The Johns Hopkins University Press, 1994) p. 114.

28 See, for example, Paul Delany and George Landow, eds. *Hypermedia and Literary Studies* (Cambridge: MIT Press, 1991) and George Landow, *Hypertext: The Convergence of Contemporary Critical Theory and Technology* (Baltimore: Johns Hopkins University Press, 1992).

29 Gregory Ulmer, p. 21.

30 Stephen Heath, 'Ambiviolences: Notes for reading Joyce,' in *Post-Structuralist Joyce. Essays from the French*, ed. by Derek Attridge and Daniel Ferrer (Cambridge: Cambridge University Press, 1984), p. 31. Further references to this edition are given after quotations in the text.

31 Jacques Derrida, 'Two words for Joyce' in Attridge and Ferrer, p. 147.

[3] Your Place or Mine? Locating Digital Art

"All that once was directly lived has become mere representation." When the French social theorist Guy Debord made this observation in 1967 he was thinking about the ways in which media saturated cultures reduced social relations to an incessant flow of images, the unfolding of "a pseudo-world apart, solely as an object of contemplation." In other words, within advanced capitalist economies lived experience had become a spectacle.[1] Within this *société du spectacle* human beings were situated as viewers of a visual language of appearances that effectively separated them from any sense of firsthand experience. Debord's spectacle immediately brings to mind Eco's hyperreality, Baudrillard's simulacrum, and more distantly, Plato's phantasm. But it also sounds very much like what we now refer to as virtuality. People living in spectacular society don't observe the mediation of their world as if they are watching a film. On the contrary, they are totally *immersed* within a visual environment that is not real, but appears as if it is. Three decades after its initial inception, the figure of the spectacle finds resonance in the emerging social formation known as virtual culture. The metaphysics of virtual culture have already passed into the realm of received ideas, a *bricolage* of neo-Platonist idealism, Cartesian dualism and Leibnizian monadology. Its fetish is the disembodied sensorium, liberated from the materiality of the body, its totem the Web, representing the decentered network of pure information. Debord's "separation *within* human beings" anticipates this culture based on disembodiment, and his notion of a "world beyond"[2] is suggestive of the abstract, artificial reality of computer generated environments that make it possible. More specifically, Debord's postulate that people are simultaneously immersed in, as well as spectators of *apparent* experience, prompts consideration of the aesthetics of virtual artifice, and in particular the question of its locality.

Like fractal geometry, digital art is endemic to the computer. While such a statement runs the risk of tautology, it serves to indicate that digital art is unthinkable without the material apparatus of the computer, a CPU and monitor, and its physical proximity to the user: while it is computer-based it is also computer-bound. Even in the case of work that is remote and accessed via the Internet, interaction with it requires an assemblage of technology that ultimately allows someone to regard a screen, sitting on their lap or on top of their desk. Drawing on Brenda Laurel's metaphor for the current state of interface design, the aesthetic experience of computer-based digital art is like watching a play performed on a proscenium stage.[3] Something is perceived that only occupies a partial place in the spectator's overall sensory environment, an exclusive *mise en scène* that is reinforced by peripheral vision and other perceptual reminders of extra-diegetic experience. While there is agency in the form of interaction, it is limited by the degree to which we can forget that our involvement is still an analogue procedure. Just as in a theater, where willing suspension of disbelief constitutes a type of immersion, our experience of computer-based digital art works by analogous identification with a *mise en scène* that is out of the realm of our sensory apprehension. I can watch the antics of Troy Innocent's *Shaolin Wooden Men*, but I can't appropriate them (much as I would like too!) As compelling as such experience can be, it hardly places the spectator in Plato's cave, for as with other art forms such as literature and film, identification can only go so far. Following the logic of virtual or apparent reality outlined above, the spectacle and the spectator are as clearly and unproblematically distinct in digital art as in other forms.

Mike Leggett's successful *Burning the Interface* (1996) exhibition, the first major survey of international CD-ROM art, declared, through the very fact of its occurrence, that digital art is still in the process of finding its place in the literal as well as cultural sense. The fact that this is digital *art* does not *a priori* determine in advance that interactives should be placed within the traditional gallery or museum. Given the cyberpunk poetics, and indeed politics of much digital art (the work of Linda Dement, or the CyberDada group, for instance), the "street" seems a more likely arena, in keeping with cyberculture's disavowal of privacy, institutional hegemony and diminution for public space (it would be a strange day, indeed, if Survival Research Laboratories were to stage *A Carnival of Misplaced Devotion* in the Museum of Modern Art, or the Tate Gallery). The relationship between digital art and the museum is a problematic one. It is clear that the very nature of digital art as an interactive, rather than contemplative form, doesn't sit well in the gallery. The time required to become involved with and navigate interactives means that its public, competitive context is not the best situation to attempt to experience it. The distraction of the crowd behind you waiting for their "turn" is the definitive essay on this topic. Exhibitions such as *Burning the Interface*, or, to a lesser degree *Cyberzone* (Melbourne, 1996) ultimately raise the question of the appropriate location of digital art, mainly because the intermediate technology required for its display does not actually need the specialized context of the gallery. Not everyone can have a Brett Whiteley in their own home, but anyone interested in the work of Troy Innocent can, potentially, explore *Idea-ON>!* in the uncompromised, domestic privacy of their own space.

As *Burning the Interface* attests, digital art is, at the moment, dependent upon the museum context to reach and create an audience, even though the nature of the work itself is often at odds with that context (on a purely practical level, a work such as David Blair's *Waxweb* is so labyrinthine and encyclopedic that even assuming you could monopolize a terminal long enough to attempt to fully explore it, you would probably need to make multiple visits to the gallery to do so). In this it revisits the complexities surrounding early electronic art of the 1950s, such as the multi-media performances of Merce Cunningham and John Cage, or the work of Nam June Paik, as well as the conceptual art of the 1960s and 1970s, represented by the minimalist sculptor Carl André. Paik's television and video installations immediately brought the domestic context into collision with the institutional ambience of canonical art. At the same time, though, his "prepared televisions" generated meanings that were conceptual, and only had meaning within the context of the gallery, since they totally disrupted television's normal function and its iconic understanding as a diversionary, every day object. In a similar reflexive vein, André's assemblages of bricks de-aestheticized the art work by confusing artspace with streetscape, disclosing the polemical insight that aesthetic value and meaning is something that is bestowed upon every day objects, quite often by their mere location within the gallery. Likewise, the collaborations between Merce Cunningham and John Cage foregrounded the role of the aleatoric in art, which they interpreted as something that "happens" anywhere, rather than something that is orchestrated and requires a special auditorium. Cage's poetics of chance operations meant that the artistic event was entirely unpredictable and showed no respect for the traditional protocols of dedicated performance spaces.

The work of Cunningham and Cage has not been given the credit it is due as the first form of electronic, multimedia art. They introduced, for example, the practice of triggering light and sound by the movements of a dancer through a spatial environment crisscrossed by sensors. The legacy of this practice can be seen in the work of the British multimedia artist Chris Hales, as well as in the *Mandala* system of "unencumbered virtual reality." This system evidences Debord's conception of the spectacle as something not only that you are in, but that you also watch yourself in. Standing in front of a blue screen, against which your silhouette is captured and fed into the virtual space on the screen in front of you, you perform actions (without the need for data-gloves and HMD) that locate you *within* the screen space in front of you. The spectator has simultaneously become the spectacle, passing beyond the screen into the virtual representation. The dialectic of inside/outside, still entrenched in computer-bound art, has started to implode.

The question of where digital art should take place inevitably invites consideration of the experience of place it generates. The most likely and desirable outcome of the trajectory of digital art from the desktop to immersive, virtual spaces, is the creation of something that resembles the Holodeck on *Star Trek: The Next Generation* or, even better, the programmable, holographic nursery in Ray Bradbury's story 'The Veldt'. In both cases the emphasis on unencumbered movement through a compellingly realistic environment evidences the principle of spectacular society that apparent reality is all around you, its ruptures difficult to identify (the nursery in the Bradbury story is complete with "odorophonics" and the simulated sun creates authentic perspiration). Of course, unlike Debord's subjects of false-consciousness, inhabitants of simulated, virtual worlds don't want to find the seams that betray the virtuality of the world they are in. Case's experience of "simstim" in William Gibson's *Neuromancer* also suggests the exhilaration offered by inhabiting that "other space" and in particular the idea of freedom of movement within it.

Complete immersion of the sensorium is still a long way off. Interactive installation art, though, offers some interesting versions of a different kind of experience of identification from computer-bound work. A 1996 installation of Graham Harwood's *Rehearsal of Memory* in Sydney focused attention on to a projected image that is remote, liberated from the small scale of the screen. With this work you become highly conscious of interacting with space, with something that is architectural, more expansive than the totality of the computer apparatus. Interactivity, in this respect, is more inclusive, adding a sense of depth to the experience that is hard to achieve when the screen is only inches away. Similarly, sculptural, prehensile interfaces, such as Agnes Hegedüs' *Handsight* (1992–93), take inclusiveness a step further by requiring that the user physically become part of the interface, by mobilizing a hand-held "eye-ball" in a transparent sphere, which in turn projects on to a screen a fantastic, probe-like journey through a world of three-dimensional objects contained in a Hungarian religious bottle, an example of virtual installation art in miniature. The other advantage of *Handsight*, contrary to its name, is that you can walk around it, maneuvering yourself

JON McCORMACK, Turbulence, 1995. Courtesy the artist.

to get the best angle of attack to explore the work's hidden secrets more closely.

Perambulation is undoubtedly an important aesthetic criterion of the virtual experience. Feeling as if you are actually chasing the White Rabbit into Wonderland, without worrying about tripping over wires, is a tantalizing notion. The idea of walking through and interacting within virtual spaces is central to the conceptual work of architects such as Marcos Novak, whose "liquid architecture" suggests a space through which things, including users, can flow. However, it has a much older lineage in the classical *ars memoria*, a practice of artificial memory designed to enable rhetoricians to recite long speeches or narratives with flawless accuracy. The elaborate memory places or *loci* designed within the mind of the orator were fabulous buildings, usually in the period style of the speaker, adorned with myriad images and objects which signified a particular piece of information to be drawn on in its correct context within the performance. The orator recited while simultaneously "walking" through this eidetic, inner place: the spectacle within. We tend to forget that digital art is all about creating what Ted Nelson has called "magic place(s) of literary memory."[4]

The idea of "the walk" through a fantastic place of memory was very much in evidence in the *Cyberzone* exhibition of Jon McCormack's seminal *Turbulence* (1995). I have seen this great work many times, but its *Cyberzone* installation was undoubtedly the most innovative, in that it extends the potential of the work to accommodate a stronger sense of a virtual experience into which one enters. This was literally suggested by the narrow entry-way, through which you walked into the darkened space defined by *Turbulence*. Through this atmospheric entrance, which resembled a portal to a kind of oddities display, complete with illuminated canisters exhibiting preserved

33

JON McCORMACK,
Turbulence, 1995.
Courtesy the artist.

specimens of what look like organic life, one was highly conscious of leaving one world behind and delving into another. The parallel here, of course, is with sideshows and ghost-train rides, which are early forms of immersive simulation (at the opening of *Cyberzone* I saw a film crew ingeniously gliding its cameraman into *Turbulence* on a wheelchair, adding another dimension to the concept of the virtual as a space of mobility). The modest graphic user interface of *Turbulence* heightened the sensation of being in an unencumbered experience, and its impact was such that you didn't necessarily have to be in command of it to feel a part of the "place" that was created within the installation space.

On the basis of this presentation of *Turbulence*, it is easy to imagine a disappearing interface, the creation of a genuinely "invocational" space, to use Chris Chesher's term, that can be activated, called into being by those "present" within it.[5] *Turbulence* is very persuasive in its evocation of a virtual place that allows one to temporarily forget that there is a world beyond. However, even *Turbulence* requires a meta-place, a location for this evocation to "take place," as was the case in an earlier, famous perambulatory environment, Myron Krueger's *Video Place* (1970). At the moment, like most computer-bound digital art, it is very much a touring exhibit that finds temporary residence in university galleries, occasional exhibitions, conferences devoted to digital art, and major state exhibitions aimed at introducing cyberculture to the general public (such as *Cyberzone*). The issue of monumentality is highly contentious within cyber circles, and it remains to be seen whether or not virtual artifice will find a home in the permanent collections of mainstream art galleries. The very ambiguity of digital art's relationship to the gallery crystallizes the original question of where it is best located. On the basis of the analogy with Debord's spectacle, it is clear that such art should be all around us, everywhere we look, which is, of course, the goal of immersive experience. As an art form dependent upon high technology, though, digital art will have to struggle, as previous avant-garde art has done, with the problematic issue of its location, even its locatability. This problematic is as interesting as the work itself and promises to be a spectacle to keep at least both eyes on.

1 Guy Debord, *The Society of the Spectacle*, trans. D. Nicholson-Smith (New York: Zone Books, 1995) p. 12.
2 Debord, p. 18.
3 Brenda Laurel, *Computers As Theatre* (Menlo Park: Addison-Wesley, 1993) p. 205.
4 Ted Nelson, *Literary Machines* (Sausalito: Mindful Press, 1993) 1/30.
5 Chris Chesher, "Aesthetics and Politics of Invocational Media," paper presented at the *New Media Forum*, Art Gallery of New South Wales, 22 October 1995, p. 3.

[4] Un Autre Coup de Dés.
Multimedia and the Game Paradigm

A century ago the great French *symboliste* Stéphane Mallarmé published his remarkable concrete poem *Un Coup de Dés* ("A throw of the dice"). Mallarmé's poem was a dramatic experiment, an attempt to materialize his interests in chance and indeterminacy in the physical, typographical layout of the printed page. He succeeded, and *Un Coup de Dés* has retained its edge in the face of impressive longevity, holding its own against the deconstructionist typography of graphic designers such as David Carson. *Un Coup de Dés* was in part a response to changing ideas about poetry and poetics, particularly in relation to the technology of the printed page. The page, as a representational field, was forced to yield new expressive possibilities under the strain of Mallarmé's inventive interpretation of the relationship between words, space and time. In his Preface to the original *Cosmopolis* edition, Mallarmé reflected on the way in which his technique dispersed, rather than transgressed, established ways of operating. Dispersal has become a focal theme in discussions of contemporary poetics, especially in relation to new media arts. Mallarmé's interest in the game of *hasard*, or throwing dice, as a way forward for poetics, finds uncanny relevance in our own *fin de siècle*, a period in which an emergent art form, multimedia, is also defining itself in relation to traditional art. Within multimedia art, too, many of the traditional forms of representation are being dispersed, rather than broken or superceded, opened up to the extended potential of virtual, networked space.

Un Coup de Dés caused quite a sensation when it was published in 1897. I'd like to think that multimedia art has the capacity to inspire in its users the same degree of excitement as that felt by Mallarmé's disciple, the poet Paul Valéry, when he first saw the poem:

> It seemed to me that I was looking at the form and pattern of a thought, placed for the first time in finite space. Here space itself truly spoke, dreamed, and gave birth to tem-

poral forms. Expectancy, doubt, consternation, all were *visible things* ... . There amid murmurs, insinuations, visual thunder, a whole spiritual tempest carried page by page to the extremes of thought, to a point of ineffable rupture—there the marvel took place, there on the very paper some indescribable scintillation of final stars trembled infinitely pure in an inter-conscious void ... I was struck dumb by this unprecedented Arrangement.[1]

Multimedia criticism has yet to reach such sublime heights, but it's very early days yet. However, the idea of chance and indeterminacy as an underlining poetic for multimedia art is attractive and appropriate. The semiotic principle of multimedia (connectionist programming) allows for, and indeed maximizes, those elements of surprise and unpredictability that so impressed Valéry. But unpredictability, as part of the creative process as well as the aesthetic experience, is nothing new to the arts. The kind of logic that has come to be associated with digital media is something with which we are already very familiar, especially within the avant-garde arts.

Our engagement with interactives is driven by the cybernetic principle of feedback, the ability of the program to respond to external input, assess those interactions, and precipitate further action on the basis of this information. Feedback, generally, assumes memory of expected outcomes within certain situations. But it also takes into account conditions of unpredictability, the assumption that information received in unexpected or new situations will yield an actual performance based entirely on that information. This behavioral contract between the responsive ecology of the computer and the agency of the user recapitulates something else with which we are familiar: the structures of games and game play; that is, two participants competing with each other strategically within a framework of contingencies. Games are dialectical in that roles are determined around the competitive dynamic of creating/overcoming obstacles that precede the achievement of a goal or outcome. They are effectively a battle for control of the flow of information, or misinformation, as the case may be. The strategies deployed within a game playing environment involve processes of adjustment and readjustment as strategic responses to the actions of an opponent. Taken together, these features of control and feedback indicate that games also fit under the general rubric of cybernetics: the science of control and communication within organic and inorganic systems.

The first theorist of game theory, as it applies to the activities of "computing machines," was Norbert Wiener. Cybernetics, as Wiener developed the idea in the 1940s, was a hybrid discipline, drawing only in part on differential switching and the theory of messages. More conspicuously, Wiener's work took great inspiration from the linguistics of Roman Jakobson and the game theory of John Von Neumann. Von

ancestralement à n'ouvrir pas la main
                              crispée
              par delà l'inutile tête

        legs en la disparition

                    à quelqu'un
                              ambigu

              l'ultérieur démon immémorial

    ayant
          de contrées nulles
                        induit
        le vieillard vers cette conjonction suprême avec la probabilité

                          celui
                              son ombre puérile
        caressée et polie et rendue et lavée
                        assouplie par la vague et soustraite
                        aux durs os perdus entre les ais

                          né
                              d'un ébat
        la mer par l'aïeul tentant ou l'aïeul contre la mer
                  une chance oiseuse

                                                  Fiançailles
      dont
            le voile d'illusion rejailli leur hantise
            ainsi que le fantome d'un geste

                          chancellera
                          s'affalera

                      folie

Neumann's *Theory of Games* was an influential text for Wiener, and can be read as the principle intertext of his *Cybernetics: Or Control and Communication in the Animal and the Machine* (1948). Von Neumann's game theory helped Wiener crystallize his central notion of entropy and the battle to control its increase within natural systems and constructed environments. The second law of thermodynamics dictates that entropy, within any closed system, such as the universe or the human body, is always on the increase (closed systems lose energy and wind down without external input). Wiener made the radical assumption that most human activity was, in one way or another, an attempt to minimize the forces of entropy. Game theory provided him with the metaphor to figure all human activity as a type of contest, an attempt to overcome resistance or keep adversarial forces at bay through the use of strategy. From a cybernetic point of view, human life was a game played against a fierce competitor, and an activity such as eating breakfast was the opening gambit in our quotidian struggle with entropy.

Wiener learned from Von Neumann that game theory was a structuralist discipline and could be applied to all social and cultural phenomena. Its principle tenet involved the notion of players, or arrangements of players, who develop a strategic approach to achieving certain ends, against specific forces or odds pitted against them. In applying cybernetics to linguistics, for example, Wiener saw that this isometric process of pressure and resistance could be used to account for the way that language works. Speech was essentially a cybernetic event, a struggle for control within communication between talkers and listeners, both battling the forces of confusion and misunderstanding. Understanding, the accurate communication of a meaning between players, was for Wiener not a qualitative achievement in itself, but a curtailing of entropy, a measurement of the degree to which misunderstanding *has not* prevailed. To complicate matters further, players within language games could consciously jam communications, thereby adding the dimension of strategy to the dramatic contest to control the flow of meaning.

Mallarmé's dice-throwing is once again instructive in this context. The complete title of the poem, *Un Coup de Dés Jamais N'Abolira Le Hasard* ("A throw of the dice will never abolish chance") suggests the futility of attempting to control contingency, to overcome chance. Words scatter and bounce hither and thither across the page, resisting hierarchy and syntactical protocols. In this way the poem is a powerful enactment of the play of meaning as something fugitive, dispersed. Reading Mallarmé is a game, a contest to wrest meaning from meaninglessness, a game that many postmodern readers still fail to win. Reading has always been a game played in the name of closure, a contest to locate meaning against the forces of entropy (meaninglessness) or superfluity (excess). A text like *Un Coup de Dés* is an important frame of reference within a discussion of new media arts because it exemplifies the ways in which so-called linear media (books) have struggled to extend beyond the confines of their apparatus. Janet Murray, in her *Hamlet on the Holodeck. The Future of Narrative in Cyberspace*, describes the ways in which certain experimental narratives broke loose of their boundaries, "like a two-dimensional picture trying to burst out of its frame."[2] Murray demonstrates how the multiform literary texts of writers such as Borges and Calvino stretched the limits of the technology of the book, and precipitated the need for a technology like the computer to capture "cascading permutations" of story-line.[3] Murray offers a convincing argument for the continued need to think of interactives as narrative situations, story spaces shaped by narrative structure, and made intelligible by the exercise of assumptions concerning narrative. In other words, narrative is very much one of the rules of the game in multimedia (indeed, narrative is structured like a game, with rules that are known, in advance, by artist and audience alike). The way in which users of interactives seek to overcome obstacles, solve puzzles and succeed in quests is evidence of the continued drive of the will to narrative within the new representational spaces made available by digital media. The pursuit of narrative is, more often than not, the Ariadne's thread that enables us to successfully navigate a world such as *Myst*. Or, from a cybernetic point of view, narrative is the means by which a player controls the increase in entropy, the forces of confusion which frustrate us at every failed attempt to make something happen in that static world. *Myst* is, in fact, a wonderful example of a closed system, a world in which nothing happens without external input.

In *Hamlet on the Holodeck*, Murray has assembled a Propp-like inventory of fundamental game structures, all of which revolve around the theme of the agon, or contest between opponents (the same economy as identified by Wiener in relation to cybernetics). This pattern of struggle and reconciliation, derived from the classical archetype of Daedalus and the Minotaur, finds expression in a range of scenarios such as the quest (*King's Quest*), the puzzle (*The Seventh Guest*), the maze (*Zork*), combat (*Doom*), and the exploration of an unfamiliar world (*Myst*). Murray is one of the first critics to offer such a structuralist critique of the array of available interactives. As with literary works, she finds that there is also considerable overlap, and any single work may contain several or all of these scenarios. It is through this interweaving of different story types that multimedia offers the potential to reconcile the tired, default opposition between the exploratory and reflective experience of literature and the adrenaline charged impact of video-arcade-style digital media. Murray refers to these experiments in a new medium as electronic juvenilia, the digital equivalent of the first books, or incunabula; that is, works of a technology in its infancy, in this case the "narrative computer."[4] They are historically important in that they combine and synthesize the contemplative, temporal aspect of narrative and the intense, sustained presence of electronic games. A bit like reading *Un Coup de Dés*, really.

A good, illustrative example of this type of work (though one not discussed by Murray) is the Residents' *Bad Day on the Midway* (Inscape, 1995). Described by the Residents as an "anti-game," involving an anti-hero, *Bad Day on the Midway* is a highly self-conscious exploration of the game as agon, a strife-ridden interaction between malevolent adversary and good-natured opponent. Like a novel, the world of the Midway is directed by characters and their stories. It is decidedly more in the manner of the later Henry James, William Faulkner and James Joyce than George Eliot or Jane Austen. There is no over-arching narrative point of view, but rather a promiscuous, peripatetic series of centers of consciousness, through which the player can vicariously move from one to the other, building up a collagic, polyphonic view of an entire world of motivation and subterfuge. The integrity of the world of the Midway and our sensation within it as an apparent reality, or time-space continuum, is heightened by the principle of feedback. Choices made by the player have an actual bearing on the unfolding of events, unlike the hokey, pseudo-choices of games such as *Quantum Gate*, which simply activate a pre-programmed algorithm. Rather than producing *expected* outcomes, gameplay yields *actual* outcomes that develop out of the idiosyncratic decision-making of any given player. This inbuilt randomness of the gameplay is a unique and powerful enhancement, sustaining the feel of a cosmos in which action precipitates causes and effects that are unique and not repeatable.

The prevailing atmosphere of *Bad Day on the Midway* is a kind of insidious miasma, an overwhelming sensation of creeping corruption and imminent danger, despite the spectacular, carnivalesque sideshows, which come alive in Jim Ludtke's inspired rendering. All the characters one encounters have their own dark agendas, and the drama of interaction involves a kind of forensic piecing together of their motivations and potential actions. This cautious, detective investigation into the psychological makeup of the characters and their respective hearts of darkness, requires considered monitoring of all the thoughts going through their minds, which are displayed, *à la* Mallarmé, sporadically across the screen as you see the world from their point of view. To keep track of their thoughts over time requires an active, diligent memory, attentive to the possible cross-overs and parallels with the thoughts of other characters as well.

Without an omniscient narrator to organise such information for us, we are really faced with a considerable task of collation and assimilation of information, which may lead to the prevention of a murder (possibly yours) or the closing down of the Midway itself. This reflective activity is offset by the distracting curiosity of exploration, which is fascinating in its own right, and the dedicated game play of the fantastic side-show attractions of the Midway itself, such as *Kill A Commie Shooting Gallery*, *Dagmar the Dog Woman*, and *Tortures Top Ten*.

Bad Day on the Midway is an excellent example of the interface between literary theories of narrative, cybernetic articulations of game theory and multimedia environments. It is suggestive of the way in which new media art is defining itself as an apparatus through the inventive grafting of elements from a range of traditional art forms on to the innovative potential of the computer. *Bad Day on the Midway* cleverly exploits the tension within gameplay between captivation and strategic reflection, engagement with the immediate task at hand and the need to keep anticipating future moves and actions. The temptation to forget about plots and strategems is considerable, as the sideshows are themselves strategically placed decoys of *divertissement*, perfidiously designed to distract the player from the pitfalls that lurk around every attraction and concession stand. This aesthetic of delay, which is fundamental to all narrative art forms, is an important rule of the game, since it disperses the idea of closure through the duration of unpredictable actions and outcomes, based entirely on choices the player makes. It reinforces the idea of the story-world as an entropic space, constantly winding down toward closure, requiring persistent suspension of the ending. Here is Norbert Wiener's contingent universe, a world in which God most certainly plays dice.

---

1 Paul Valéry, quoted in Stéphane Mallarmé, *Collected Poems*, trans. H. Weinfield (Berkeley: University of California Press, 1994) p. 265.

2 Murray, J, *Hamlet on the Holodeck. The Future of Narrative in Cyberspace* (New York: Free Press, 1997) p. 28.

3 ibid., p. 38.

4 ibid., pp. 28–9.

[5] Travelling to *Iconica*:
The Virtual Worlds of Troy Innocent

In the world of interactive media no one has a monopoly on mutation. From William Latham's *Chimera & Chromosomes* to Jon McCormack's *Turbulence*, unnatural selection has provided some vivid and memorable spectacles of cyber sculptural, artificial life. It is not surprising to find that transmutation is *de rigueur* in multimedia art, for the prevailing rhetoric of digital aesthetics points to the recombinant aspect of *multi-* and *inter-*media as a way of conceptualizing and defining the kind of art that ought to be produced by such cultural technologies. However this rhetoric runs counter to the more speculative consideration of critics such as Steven Holtzman, who, in his book *Digital Mantras. The Languages of Abstract and Virtual Worlds*, asks the question, "What visual worlds of expression will we consider to be idiomatic to computers?"[1] A fair question, given that we may not yet be in a position to recognize such worlds when we see them, for as Holtzman argues the illusionism of digital space is still motivated by a desire for *trompe-l'oeil* realism (he locates computer graphic imaging directly in the tradition of Brunelleschi, Alberti and the techniques of vanishing-point perspective). An awful lot of computer-generated art does seem, though, to have fallen prey to the chimaerical imperative, the prescriptive urge to be "way weird" for its own sake. Ovid, classical author of the *Metamorphoses*, may well have been the theoretician of animation, as Hugh Kenner has suggested. It doesn't follow, however, that multimedia should automatically claim him as its demiurge.

While the emergent field of multimedia art is already showing signs of fatigue from this unspoken inheritance, the fatigue of store-bought artifice, software-driven creativity and abundant self-similarity, a number of artists have emerged from the flurry of activity of the last five years whose work bears the unmistakable inflections of difference, ingenuity, and an astute understanding of the medium. The work of Melbourne-based artist Troy Innocent stands out from the crowd by virtue of its overwhelming integrity as great *art*, regardless of the fact that it is made using a computer. In Troy Innocent, digital animation may well have found its first major exponent of the art of virtuality, for his work inventively responds to the challenge to find a visual, expressive language that is truly unique to computers. Innocent's work is one of the best examples we have of what Ken Wark has called the "new abstraction," the development of new structures of signifying relations and systems of figuration apposite to the electronic age. Remember this is a space of abstraction we're talking about, "there's no there, there." Perhaps we need to start thinking of new media artists as translators, mediators between the virtual and the real.

Troy Innocent has spent the last ten years travelling in the virtual world, and his impressive body of work is a travelogue of his journeys through the strange topographies of cyberspace. His early collaborative work with the CyberDada collective in Melbourne (Dale Nason, Elena Popa) established the conceptual frameworks for the abstract virtual spaces and unique iconographic signscapes that have become his idiom: a nightglow blend of tumescent body culture, ingenious mutational assemblages made up of flesh, mechano-bits and jelly beans, and elaborate spectacles of consumption (the term *menu* acquires a very specific meaning in the *Innocent GUI*). His films, *Jawpan*, and with Elena Popa *Noodle Film* and *Techno Digesto Fetishism*, graphics and interactives, *Iconworld*, *Idea-ON>!*, *Nano in NewSOS* (with Elena Popa), have been exhibited regularly at SIGGRAPH, ISEA, as well as major galleries such as the Tate (Liverpool), and other international symposia devoted to new media arts. With cybernetic body-artist Stelarc, he developed the STIMBOD touchscreen interface, which allows the user to interact remotely with human reflex circuitry (this project is an extension of his interest in souped-up flesh, charged with electricity or saccharine). He is also a collaborator with the world's first simulated recording group, the Shaolin Wooden Men, who have two collections of techno music to their name (they have informed me, via the noodlesphere, that Innocent is, in fact, their invention).

Indeed, recognizing that collaboration and communication are intrinsic to the effectiveness of computer interactivity, Innocent's interfaces have all emerged through working with others. Whether simply testing interactive designs for their ability to communicate or creating works such as *Techno Digesto Fetishism*, in which he, Elena Popa and Dale Nason each produced forms that cannibalized other images, Innocent has noted how collaboration has allowed him to "develop components of language."

During this time of exploration to the new worlds of cyberspace, Innocent has mastered its languages, establishing himself as the first philologist of virtual reality. His

initial sorties into the digital universe are elaborate architectures of information, pre-linguistic
signscapes that, like hieroglyphics, tantalize with
the look of a profound significance that is just
out of reach, mystic ciphers awaiting the key that
will unlock their secrets. Innocent intuited very
early that these languages were clearly intelligent and suggested that a complex ecology of
artificial life existed "on the other side of reality."
Moreover, its inhabitants were doing their best to
speak to us. Like Jean-François Champollion, the
first person to successfully decipher Egyptian
hieroglyphics, Innocent needed a Rosetta Stone,
a key to communicating the experience of being
digital. He found this in *Idea-ON>!* (1992-1994),
an audacious, interactive log of his voyage into
the mythic dreamscape of that ecology. On this
trip he captured its rituals, sacred sites, pleasure
gardens and modes of communication. In this
"cybaroque world" he found a "surreal kind of
logic," a realm of abstraction and mutation that
he continues to map. Described as a "Database
of Experience," or series of "prototypes for virtual worlds," the five environments of *Idea-ON>!*
possess their own ambience and idiosyncratic
populace of knowbots, super deformed cuties,
noodleboys and iconbods. However they share a
common theme of synthetic space, "a dreamlike,
surreal, communal cyberspace in which the perception of synthetic media reality is recon-
structed/mutated." Although Innocent regards
the work as "a little old now," it still impresses
with the force of inspired, pioneering creativity in
a new medium. *Idea-ON>!* is an experimental
essay on the nature of computer art, a "direct response to the potential of interactive technologies

TROY INNOCENT, Idea-ON>! 1992–94.
Courtesy the artist.

45

and the concept of virtual reality. It was also a kind of expression of forms, images and places from my subconscious manifested inside the computer, using the 'natural' aesthetic of computer graphics." As part of the *Burning the Interface* exhibition held at the Museum of Contemporary Art in Sydney in 1996, *Idea-ON>!* was the *punctum* that shot out from that multimedia landscape.

In these worlds Innocent has cataloged a veritable bestiary of artificial life, from the super deformed cuties and knowbots of *Jawpan* and *Idea-ON>!*, to the more intelligently amplified Shaolin Wooden Men. The Shaolin Wooden Men made their first appearance in 1994 as a manifestation of sound, in the guise of a self-titled CD of techno-music. The Shaolin Wooden Men are without doubt the first artists to have come out of cyberspace and tour the real world, giving audiences their first taste of art produced by "mind children" (the name given by roboticist Hans Moravec to the artificial progeny of human-interface technology). Their elaborate multimedia performances record the unique image-soundscape of the electronic world, opening up the interactive gateway through which we can enter into their world (I have been prevented by their front man and vocalist, "Special Go Man," to say anything about their forthcoming and long-awaited anthem of the datasphere, "Cyberspace Truckin'").

More than a designer of virtual worlds, Innocent has developed expertise in "speaking" their languages, which are essentially audiovisual. The digital does constitute a language of sorts, conducted on an infravisible, inhuman level. Innocent's work is remarkable in that he has created an extensive, virtual cosmography, an image-sphere that interprets digital code as elementary quanta, the quark, strangeness and charm of beautifully rendered multisensory realities. This synthesis of visual sign-systems, iconography and their associated acoustic equivalents, suggests that like our own phonetic alphabet, these languages involve a sophisticated interplay of the senses. This is why multimedia is rapidly becoming the standard human-computer interface. To engage intelligently with artificial lifeforms we must learn their multisensory languages, since such languages promise to extend our limited understanding of the human-computer interface. This is a language that goes beyond the flatness of the computer screen and true type font. It is an ambient language that takes place in space and time.

PsyVision (1996), Innocent's inspired music-video collaboration with the Shaolin Wooden Men and the *Psy-Harmonics* techno music label, eloquently demonstrated the communicational power of such fusions of the senses. Innocent's cyberdelic, trippy graphics have been associated with the Melbourne rave/dance scene for a number of years and have come to stand as a talisman for its pretensions to techno-induced nirvana. However, it would be a mistake to assume that Innocent's latest work is merely a visual accompaniment to the techno-mantra. Described as a "fusion of iconic figuration and synthetic abstraction towards a language for the visual expression of techno music," *PsyVision* is a multi-sensory exploration of the visual representation *of* techno. Don't you wonder sometimes, about sound and vision? David Bowie asked that question on his *Low* album of 1977. Around the same time I remember listening to Klaus Schulze's proto-techno album *Blackdance* and wondering what it would *look* like, and no doubt a similar intrigue prompted Innocent in his engagement with techno. Like Mark Dery, who in his *Escape Velocity. Cyberculture at the End of the Century* asks a similar question in relation to cyberpunk fiction, Innocent is interested in creating an "objective correlative,"[2] a visual language of abstract spaces, objects, and events that embody the structures and rhythms of techno. Attempting to create "a 'natural' place for this music to reside," Innocent has generated a kind of virtual data-sphere-cum-karaoke-space, in which "figures and forms become 'visual instruments' whose actions and movements are played in sequence like music." The ubiquitous Shaolin Wooden Men, who first appeared in 1994 *as* a self-titled CD of electronic music, are the emblematic avatars of this fusion of sound and vision. They describe themselves as "super deformed media constructs existing in the abstraction of electronic space," "bodies made of 'tonal frequencies.'" However, their most famous tag, "We are sound," succinctly points to the interface between sound and visual space that is central to *PsyVision*, whereby the "structures of frequencies and vibrations that make up sound can be represented through abstract computer generated geometry."

TROY INNOCENT, Shaolin Wooden Men, from *PsyVision*, 1996. Courtesy the artist.

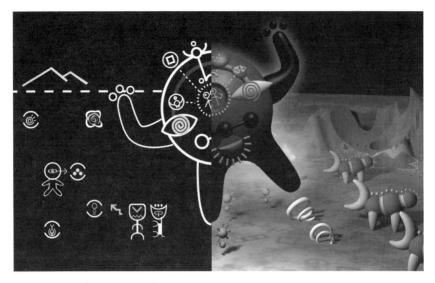

TROY INNOCENT, Iconica, 1998. Courtesy the artist.

In this way, figures such as Shaolin Wooden Man #3 (in "Ohar") and Special Go-Man function as "navigational devices facilitating the experience of sound."

PsyVision, as Innocent describes it, "represents a set of prototypical language elements for the visual expression of this new sound. Elements of this language include textures, spaces, icons, movement, colours and animated figures which are extruded into the abstract three-dimensional space of the computer." As an exploration of the fusion of "communication and digital semiotics," *PsyVision* is an important contribution to our understanding of eidetics, the visual representation of abstract data as geometric spectacles of light (a central theme of cyberpunk fiction and virtual reality interface technology). Innocent's iconic figuration of sound reinforces Philip Brophy's oft quoted adage that visual media are made up of 100% image and 100% sound (contrary to the views of the wilful, artificially intelligent Shaolin Wooden Men, who see themselves as 25% image, 12% code, 60% digital sound and 3% unknown).

Blurring the tentative membranes that mark off one form of abstraction from another, *PsyVision* is a hybrid mix of installation art, music video, psychedelic phosphotron and virtual reality experience. The various imaginary spaces represented in the eleven sections draw on a range of symbolic forms and visual dynamisms, from fractal geometries, kaleidoscopic pulses and fantastic landscapes to info-overload collage, textural "soft spaces" and liquid architectures. All these spaces are uncompromisingly synthetic, and there are no illusory pretensions to resemble any known world. Innocent certainly imitates real world textures, such as wood, plastic and metal, and there is something absolutely gorgeous about the sheen and glimmer of such surfaces: a legacy of his CyberDada collaborations, which parodied the "personal computer's clinically smooth recreation of reality." The overwhelming sensation is of "plastic beauty" (to use a phrase of Mandelbrot's) since we never for a moment doubt their artificiality. They are what Katherine Hayles calls "skeuomorphs,"[3] simulated textural realities that aren't functional, but are only required to perform the look of a particular thing that finds a new meaning in its current context ("scanned driftwood" in the case of the simulacral Shaolin Wooden Men). The simulated icing on his "rigorous" donut looks just too good to be true, the ideal form of what an iced donut should look like. But that's just the point about skeuomorphs and virtual worlds: ideal forms are abundantly commonplace. Plato would look upon Innocent's world of skeuomorphic being and see that it is good.

As far from sensory overload as you can get, Innocent's fusion of sound and image involves a complex feedback loop of the senses that sustains an ongoing "psychic harmony" of visual/auditory synchronicity. In this he has successfully achieved the philosopher's stone of cybercultural art, synaesthesia. According to *Mondo 2000's User's Guide to the New Edge* (the *dernier cri* in matters cybercultural), synaesthesia is defined as "a merging or parallelism of sensory input where pieces of information occupy the same pencils of sensory space. Sound and light might merge at the same point of data– occupying the same piece of meaning." Virtual reality environments are being designed on the premise of a holistic integration of the senses, an alchemical project that sages of VR refer to as Intelligence Amplification. The impact of Innocent's work, in this respect, is derived from its breakdown of oppositions between the senses, and its fusion of powerful singularities anchored in terms of the sensory gestalt of what film theorist Stephen Heath has called the "optical listen." In this Innocent has revolutionized both interface design (how we perceive, relate to and interact with computer generated entities and realities), and the aesthetics of technoculture: What-You-See-Is-What-You-Hear.

Consistent with the cosmographical integrity of his earlier work, *PsyVision* generates a strong sense of internal wholeness. Everything we encounter in each of the different environments seems right, and nothing is out of place; we should expect nothing less than to eavesdrop on the Shaolin Wooden Men recording their 1994 self-titled album in their studio/temple. As with any closed-system (cybernetic, social or artistic), Innocent's synaesthetic world functions according to the principle of infinite variation within a finite set, the recurrence of elements and figures that not only seem, intuitively, to belong, but which we have also seen before. In fact, there is a strong sense of the uncanny in Innocent's work, the sensation that his worlds are strangely familiar. Part of this is due to his embossing and remapping of different, sometimes ancient cultures on to the iconic forms of cyberspace (a project of "sampling and reconstruction" he traces back to earlier work, such as *Jawpan*). The visual imagery of Japanese noodle commercials, Zen Buddhism, Islamic asceticism, pagan Earth worship and Koori land art all feature as readymades of multi-cultural memory, and find a new place and a new identity in the Utopia of his virtual geographies. The overlapping or colliding of different elements is part of an overall aesthetic goal to "avoid a generic 'computer graphic look,' as generated by Microsoft or the Apple CHI guidelines, by using tools in experimental ways, and combining many different tools together, to create a form of personal expression for myself in the computer. At the same time, I have still tried to use and develop the unique aesthetic qualities of computer graphics, and in some cases parody or subvert them by using them in new ways."

As with all abstract art, forms and shapes within Innocent's figurative spaces interrelate with each other in fundamental and profound ways, every item signifying its place as a lexical item in a synthetic language comprised of sound and image. His iconic figurines bear geometric and textural resemblance to each other, as well as to their forbears in previous works (especially *Jawpan* and *Idea-ON>!*), but no two are the same. The self-referential traces of semiobotic DNA reveal a genetic string of beguiling simplicity. These three-dimensional, glimmering cyber-munchkins also have their two dimensional counterparts in the form of entrancing ciphers, cabalistic articulations of digital experience: the "language of machines." Among his many contributions to the vocabulary of multi-media art, Innocent has with these symbols effectively invented a new register of pictorial sign, androglyphs, which he describes as "ancient symbols in a new world." At once invoking pictographic writing and mass-produced icons of the information age, this unique and distinctive form of hieroglyphics has started the ball rolling towards the creation of a visual language for virtual worlds, a language that falls somewhere between the digital unconscious and communication, artifice and expedience.

PsyVision formed the basis of Innocent's most recent work, *Iconica* (1998), which is the culmination of a two year work in progress that has transmogrified through such exhibited incarnations as *Memetic Mutations* (1996) and *Memespace* (1997). "*PsyVision* was the first stage of a larger idea. In a way, I am only starting to get to what I originally set out to do. Most of my previous work has been a kind of intuitive reaction to the medium, and an exploration of its potential." *Iconica* extends important, key themes from Innocent's previous work: the links between image, sound and movement, alternate realities and the ability to deform them, and the creation of unpredictable "intelligent" spaces filled with artificial, media-constructed life-forms that respond to the interactions of the user.

In this sense *Iconica* is, in its own way, a stage in Innocent's digital journey, a port of call in his exploration of a disappearing interface. The eventual construction of an "augmented reality, where the datasphere of the computer is projected out into the real world," promises to open up "a much wider band of communication between people and virtual environments" by using human gesture and speech to interact with the projected images. Until this technology is developed to a more sophisticated level, Innocent is tackling the "point and click" mode of interaction head-on, and not before time, for it has become one of the most hackneyed conventions of multimedia art. "Interaction has to be more than pressing pixelated buttons on a two-dimensional surface. Elements of video game interaction and virtual reality will be used to construct an entire environment within the computer which offers many different modes of interaction. You may converse with creatures, feed them icons, navigate the space, move

TROY INNOCENT, Iconica, 1998. Courtesy the artist.

objects around, all via direct interaction with the world itself, rather than through text-based menu systems." Currently, *Iconica* is a dual screen installation, comprising a verticular screen and horizontal, topographical bas-relief map, with which one navigates through the various environments. This manifold structure offers a kind of double vision, a way of looking at the world from two points of view: the limited, specific focus on a particular environment and an omniscient, synoptic perspective of the entire world.

Again incorporating the music of "techno wizard" Ollie Olsen (co-founder of *Psy-Harmonics* and one of the producers of *PsyVision*), *Iconica* is an elaborate extension of Innocent's synaesthetic experiments, in which the fusion of sound and image will be a central feature. He is also attempting to introduce into this work elements that, so far, have eluded even the most sophisticated experiments in multimedia, such as randomness, contingency and causal interactivity: "There is no beginning or end to the experience, and it is different every time." A "surreal, 3D version of SIMCITY," *Iconica* also takes the user into the fourth dimension, with an interface that provides the opportunity to experience the changes and effects that emerge out of interaction with the creatures that inhabit its worlds, once contact with them has been established, that is. "In order to interact more deeply, the user will need to learn at least one of the languages of these creatures, which will enable an ongoing communication with them."

Iconica is Innocent's most advanced articulation of the language of *terra* digitalis. In *Iconica* we experience the full morphology of cyberspace and its language; its lexicon of forms, its grammar, syntax, and tone. We also encounter the various dialects which mutate from the basic linguistic structure, signalling the different entities and their regional localities. In this it displays all the traits and integrity of a self-contained world. It is founded upon principles of creation and regulation familiar to us from some of the most important ideas and disciplines of knowledge relating to cosmology, artificial life and complex systems; notably, cybernetics (the science of regulation and control in machines and humans), quantum mechanics (a theory of light and its unpredictablility), and chaos theory (the study of the conditions required for matter and energy to spontaneously assemble into systems of organization). Chaos theory tells us that beyond a certain threshhold of complexity random activity will organize itself into order and become self-regulating, manifesting what chaoticians call "emergent behavior." The artificial entities in *Iconica* organize themselves into entities from elemental forms (head, heart, digestive tract). Different "inflection values" act as modifiers, which produce subtle variations in their overall composition, as well as unique and potentially infinite permutations of the available, finite set of elements within any given space. This is the unpredictability principle of quantum mechanics, the notion that light particles are fundamentally unstable and always travel in a dynamic state prone to change (these creatures are, after all, made of light). Quarks, the most elementary particles of light, are not neutral, but are "top" or "bottom," "strange," or "charmed." Like quarks, which can form themselves into unusual particles, these lifeforms cross-fertilize and mutate, quite independently of anyone or anything outside their own environment. Artificial life will find a way.

Like any dynamic process of interaction, the longer *Iconica* runs its course the more likely it is that life-like forms of organization will spontaneously occur. This process is augmented by the various interactions of different users, which transforms the entire space and time of the installation-event into a complex, self-regulating system. Any given user will produce subliminal yet profound changes in its ecology, since different users will come into the world at a specific, yet always critical moment of artificial world time, when who knows what could be happening. This non-linear, asynchronous interface means that unpredictability will prevail. The great attraction of returning to the installation at different times is to monitor how things change, to observe which spaces have been colonized by invaders, to see what new hybrids have been cross-bred and which lifeforms have been unnaturally selected for extinction.

The cybernetic principle of feedback suggests that artificial intelligence will learn from changes in its environment; the cyborg in *Terminator 2* only needs to be shown once where the ignition key is hidden. The entities of *Iconica* seem to learn about concepts such as territoriality, survival of the fittest and power. When one type of entity devours another, it acquires exotic forms which augment it in some way, which, through breeding, leads to even more bizarre hybrids and an overall proliferation of lifeforms (it's starting to sound more and more like the Galapagos Islands). They also associate acts of kindness (giving them food, talking to them) with particular users, thereby adding memory to their vital statistics.

Iconica is no simple illustration of these concepts. It is, as its name suggests, a multimedia environment composed of signs and structures of meaning. In *Iconica* Innocent has gone beyond digital animation, as it is narrowly understood. He has created a space of intelligent artificial life, of mutation and unnatural selection governed by laws of homeostasis and contingency. *Iconica* is a continuous, real-time spectacle of what chaos-theorists call singularities, transitional moments when the artificial manifests life-like behaviour. That's about as close to real life as you can hope to get in a synthetic world. And this is surely the test of any virtual world. When the map covers the territory, and the difference between the two is subliminal, you know the tide is turning. With *Iconica* it has already turned. In Innocent's next interactive *we* will in all probability be the spectacle of a quizzical audience of mind children, piqued by the merest suggestion of our autonomy. A hybrid of genres from computer simulation, electronic art and other new media such as role-playing games, *Iconica* promises to take Troy Innocent and multimedia into previously unexplored territories– providing the Shaolin Wooden Men don't get there first.

1 Steven Holtzman, *Digital Mantras: The Languages of Abstract and Virtual Worlds* (Cambridge, Mass.: MIT Press, 1994) p. 251.
2 Mark Dery, *Escape Velocity: Cyberculture at the End of the Century* (New York: Grove Press, 1996) p. 90.
3 N. Katherine Hayles, "Boundary Disputes: Homeostasis, Reflexivity, and the Foundations of Cybernetics," in Robert Markley, ed. *Virtual Realities and Their Discontents* (Baltimore: Johns Hopkins University Press, 1996) p. 16.

[6] Parallactic Readings: Joyce, Duchamp and the Fourth Dimension

I was recently doing some research on the history of mirrors when I realized that one of the books I had consulted was the *Anglo-American Cyclopaedia*, the same text referred to by Borges in "Tlon, Uqbar, Orbius Tertius." Wedged in between pages 601 and 602, I discovered a number of torn notesheets which were covered in a small, spidery writing that seemed vaguely familiar. On closer inspection I realized, to my utter astonishment, that I had found a number of Joyce's early sketches for *Ulysses*. Tracing echoes in subsequent transmissional documents and published editions, I found that all but one of the four sketches had been incorporated, either verbatim or in some augmented or developed form. Indeed, subsequent forensic research indicated that the outstanding six-line fragment, with the word "gnomon" written on the back, was not present in any of the extant notebooks available for consultation in the holdings of the British Library and the Lockwood Memorial Library (State University of New York at Buffalo). I could only conjecture that this note sheet, clearly torn from the kind of waistcoat-sized pad described by Frank Budgen,[1] must be a relic of the lost 12 kilogram bundle of unused notes which Joyce described to Myron Nutting in 1923.[2] As for its content, the anomalous fragment involved Stephen's brief recollection (its rhythm reminiscent of the initial style) of a discussion with an unnamed Parisian artist about the latter's project for an innovative work of art in glass, which broke away from the prevailing fashions of the time. Was this mysterious figure a fictional prototype of a modern iconoclast, or did Joyce actually have someone in mind? With the aid of the genetic scenario provided by Michael Groden and Rodney Wilson Owen,[3] I confidently dated the fragment as being composed around 1914, possibly from the same period as the Trieste notebook. Further historical research into the European artistic climate of the time has led me to assume that the artist in question is Marcel Duchamp, and the anticipated work is none other than *The Large Glass*.

Duchamp commenced his early, preliminary work for *The Large Glass* in Munich in 1912, and most of the voluminous working notes he wrote for it at this initial stage were made between 1913 and 1915.[4] There is no reference made to a meeting with Duchamp in Ellmann or any other of the standard accounts of Joyce's European peregrinations around this time, nor within the vast body of Joyce scholarship have I been able to find much in the way of a Joyce/Duchamp connection. Where and when Joyce might have met Duchamp, or how he came to be aware of the genesis of *The Large Glass*, are matters entirely open to speculation. The conclusion I have drawn from my startling find is that along with *The Odyssey*, *Hamlet*, and *Don Giovanni*, we need to add *The Bride Stripped Bare by Her Bachelors, even* to the list of *Ulysses* intertexts.

The compositional histories of both *Ulysses* and *The Large Glass* are uncannily synchronous; early development around 1914, consolidation during the years of the Great War, and the problematic irresolution of completion in the early 1920s (as many critics have noted, Joyce stopped writing *Ulysses*, rather than achieved textual closure, in 1922, and in 1923 Duchamp declared *The Large Glass* "definitively unfinished."[5]) A "quest for quiddities"[6] found resonances in Stephen's "cracked looking glass," and "shattering glass and toppling masonry." As well, extra-diegetic metaphors describing *Ulysses* in the early 1920s elicited the connection, such as Virginia Woolf's likening of Joyce's achievement to a man smashing open a window to breathe.[7] (Duchamp frequently referred to himself as a "breather" rather than an artist.) However, the intertextual motivation of *The Large Glass* is different from the architectonic structure of *The Odyssey*, or the thematic texturing of *Hamlet*. More dramatically, *The Large Glass* acts as a heuristic device designed to foreground the complex dialectic between composition and decomposition in the writing and reading of *Ulysses*. It prompts, in other words, the kind of attention that has occupied textual editors and the like for the last seventy years, which has disseminated the text into fragments, individual passages, individual words. Criticism of *Ulysses* has unwittingly enacted this dialectic in its undoing of our acquired understandings and critical habits, which, as Harry Levin has noted,[8] increasingly sought interpretive teleologies and holistic maps of the Joycean compositional process. Just as Duchamp eventually made multiples, replicas of *The Large Glass*, which undermined the concept of an original, master work, Joyce produced variants, thousands of them, which have increasingly drawn the attention of critics to their particularity.

Duchamp noted of *The Large Glass* that he "did not intend to make a picture to be looked at;" it was rather a "catalogue of ideas," to be thought about in relation to his working notes.[9] A few of these were published as early as 1914, but the majority were

left: James Joyce, 1915. Courtesy the Harley Croessman Collection, Morris Library, University of Southern Illinois, Carbondale.
right: Marcel Duchamp, 1917, photograph by Edward J. Steichen. Philadelphia Museum of Art: The Louise and Walter Arensberg Collection.

published in a limited facsimile form in 1934, in an edition known as *The Green Box* — a collection of 93 notes on torn pieces of loose paper in a green suede cardboard box. No mere adjunct to the *Glass*, *The Green Box* was to be consulted while looking at it. The idea that "the Glass... should be accompanied by a text of 'literature' as amorphous as possible, which never took form," enabled the spectator to think of the Glass from all possible "associative angles."[10] This evidenced Duchamp's conviction that the spectator makes the work of art through active participation, through the linking of ideas; indeed, for Duchamp the spectator was the missing link "in the chain of reactions accompanying the creative act."[11]

Duchamp told Anais Nin in 1934 that *The Green Box* represented a form that should hereafter replace finished books: "It's not the time to finish anything. It's the time of fragments."[12] In the same year an early commentator noted of *The Green Box* that "reader and spectator must find a new manner of attachment to each other, and to the problem called culture."[13] This is a useful directive of how we need to re-conceptualize *Ulysses*, for in looking at it through *The Large Glass* we can establish a new order of relation between Joyce's "continuous manuscript text"[14] and the 1922 edition. If we attend to the observations of textual theorists such as Jerome McGann, or critical theorists such as Stephen Heath,[15] we need to think of the Shakespeare and Company edition as one possible (that is Joyce's) arrangement or assemblage of an indeterminate number of potential combinations (multiples) of the thousands of notes, sketches and drafts Joyce composed in Trieste and Zurich (just as *The Large Glass* is Duchamp's construction of his own working notes). As Frank Budgen observed, "No one knew how all this material was given place in the completed pattern of his work, but from time to time in Joyce's flat one caught glimpses of a few of those big orange-coloured envelopes that are one of the glories of Switzerland, and these I always took to be the storehouses of building material."[16] The textual aporias noted over the last ten years, especially the indeterminacies generated by Joyce's notorious correction of proof, substantiate Budgen's impression of an unknowable morphology responsible for the transformation of these notes into Joyce's drafts for each episode, and eventually the published edition. Even more suggestive, especially in the light of *The Green Box*, or Duchamp's *Boite-en-Valise* (his portable museum), is the image of thousands of "stray bits of paper" crammed into an envelope, or, as he described to John Quinn, a "small valise."[17] Imagine *Ulysses* appearing on 2nd February, 1922 in a large, peacock-green envelope or suede box, with no guidance (other than a title), on what to do with all those notes. Early reviews would oscillate between bewilderment and fascination:

> He calls it a book, but it is a book such as the publishing world has not seen before... the book is not really a book but a box, and not really a box but a book. A thing to surprise to keep you guessing... The package is like a closed door, yet somehow inviting you to open it. The inside is even more surprising... (scraps of paper) as loose and free as air, money or sin, are irresponsibly beneath the hand to be read or scrutinized as you wish – no binding, no numbering, no indicated sequence. They exist, in fact, at liberty without traditional moorings.[18]

Joyce's schema would, of course, have helped, providing you were privy to leaked information from the chosen few who, until Stuart Gilbert included them in his 1930 study, were privileged to see them. (Duchamp's notes were not published in a widely available commercial edition until 1959, though in 1935 André Breton published his "Lighthouse of the Bride," a descriptive essay offering itself as an "Ariadne's thread" through *The Green Box*.) Joyce's anxiety over the possible publication of his schema with the American edition of *Ulysses* evidences his desire, like Duchamp, to sustain the reader's interactivity with his material, to suggest and stimulate acts of discovery, not to prescribe them. Duchamp's notes in his *Green Box* were not designed to enable the spectator to decode the iconography of *The Large Glass* in the name of the father, and Joyce also took precautions against overly assisting the reader (removing Homeric episode headings being a famous instance of this). The putative authorial guidance of the schemata has also been questioned by critics such as Phillip Herring, and it is instructive to think of them as being part of the overall package, like Duchamp's photographs and his explanatory accounts of sections of the *Glass*. This information may well be given; knowing what to do with it, how to relate it to an overall understanding of the *Glass*, or to construct a sythesized *Ulysses* from a sum of its parts, is another matter. Parallactic readings of *The Green Box* assume that while the number of documents to be negotiated are finite, the conditions of negotiation are not. With *Ulysses*, too, parallax becomes the necessary constitutent of a textuality that is relative, conjugate; my *Ulysses*, your *Ulysses*, his *Ulysses*, her *Ulysses*, their *Ulysses*. Discussions of the Arranger, ever since David Hayman coined the term in 1970, portray an internal, organizing presence forging self-referentiality. Thus, Hugh Kenner refers to the book's "memory-bank" to describe an organizing consciousness that "lets escape from its scrutiny the fall of no sparrow."[19] But can we divorce this assertion, which is anterior to reading, from Kenner's own collation of details produced, presumably, by many readings? As Jonathan Culler has noted, there "are no moments of authority and points of origin except those which are retrospectively designated as origins."[20] Parallax suggests that new readers, sufficiently free from critical overload, will establish their own cross-referential chains, relying, perhaps, on the Arranger as a more self-conscious

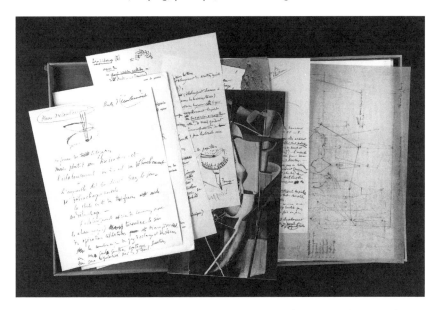

MARCEL DUCHAMP, The Green Box (*La Mariée mise à nu par ses célibataires, même*), 1934. Philadelphia Museum of Art: The Louise and Walter Arensberg Collection.

ULYSSES: The Green Box,
Darren Tofts.

form of cueing. Like a child's memory game, collation, the assimilation of contiguity, relies on the player's recognition that an element has in fact been repeated.

To conceptualize *Ulysses* in this form is to defamiliarize the dramatic, rather than epic activity of reading that Joyce no doubt had in mind for his readers; a prospect apparently only now available to new readers equipped with an ideal immunity to Joyce criticism. For the initiated, this is a Utopian prospect, for it offers an engagement with *Ulysses* that has been denied through decades of HCE (heavy critical exegesis). *Ulysses: The Green Box* edition raises important questions about how we have learned to, or been taught to read *Ulysses*. But it also occasions a revision of our sense of the phenomenology of reading, of where we are when we engage with formless conglomerations of signs. Sifting through *Ulysses: The Green Box*, where Joyce's schematic and reflexive clues are just so many fragments among others, with no signposted hermeneutic privilege, is to enter fourth dimensional space.

Writing is a mnemonic technology. It holds words still, and purportedly brings meaning to presence for immediate recollection. However *Ulysses: The Green Box* requires the exercise of an extended or virtual memory, since it lacks the spatial contiguities we normally expect writing to possess, or at least make possible. For Duchamp also the fourth dimension meant something more dynamic than the cubist notion of "the immensity of space eternalizing itself in all directions at any given moment." The fourth dimension was an ongoing activity of "interplication,"[21] the folding and unfolding of ideas as a sequence of anachronous moments, where remembered associations coalesce with newly formed combinations; hence his curious subtitle for *The Bride*

Stripped Bare by Her Bachelors, even— "delay in glass." A fourth dimensional icon such as Jan Metzinger's tea-cup (from the painting *Tea Time*) offers the illusion of a homogenous totality of numerous viewings of the object from all conceivable angles. Fourth dimensional pictorial space was poetic, a static simulation of the shifting mobility essential to human perception of objects in the natural world, as theorized by Adolf von Hildebrand. Looking at *The Large Glass* put this concept into play, concentrating the aesthetic experience as an intransitive process of incompletion, of delay, of "indecisive reunion."[22]

In this sense, Joyce and Duchamp did not produce texts, they provided systems of prompting, the primary node in an interface completed by the spectator. The nomenclature of hypermedia seems more relevant to modernist experiments in fourth dimensional space than contemporary interactive culture, of which Joyce is frequently cited as an antecedent. Derrida was quick to recognize this as the first generation of personal computers were appearing in the early 1980s. Hypermedia simulates "joyceware"[23] as Derrida foresaw over a decade ago, and that recognition returns us more agog to the prodigious fourth dimensional space that was the mind of Joyce. We return armed with new descriptive terms, their relevance pre-ordained rather than appropriated. Joyce's method of composing *Ulysses* was virtual, revising, improving, connecting and creating "all at the one time."[24] His notesheets reveal a form of shorthand (Larbaud called it "abbreviated") whereby a single word or phrase, underlined in coloured pencil, signified more expansive, amplified constructions in the author's mind.[25] Derrida's word for this, "hypermnesia," describes the Joycean interface well, an invitation to interactivity which "a priori indebts you, and in advance inscribes you in the book you are reading."[26] Every time I highlight a link when using hypertext I can't help but feel that it is quoting Joyce. Similarly, when Myron Krueger made the observation last year that hypertext liberates the reader "to make decisions about order of presentation that the author was not willing to make,"[27] I thought he was referring to the Green Boxes of Joyce and Duchamp. Cyberpunk novelist William Gibson recalled *The Bride Stripped Bare* in *Neuromancer*; perhaps *Ulysses: The Matrix* edition will turn up in a subsequent novel.

Postscript. After completing this paper I reflected on the historical dissemination of *Ulysses*. I fancied that the next stage of this process would be intertextual, the intrusion of a fabulatory *Ulysses* into the regime of available editions. If my forecast is not in error, someone may at some time in the future find the contents of this green box which I found in a second-hand bookshop, beneath a pile of encyclopedias.

1 Frank Budgen, *James Joyce and the Making of Ulysses* (London: Grayson, 1934) pp. 176–7.

2 Cited in Richard Ellmann, *James Joyce* (New York: Oxford University Press, 1981) p. 558.

3 Michael Groden, *Ulysses in Progress* (Princeton: Princeton University Press, 1977). Rodney Wilson Owen, *James Joyce and the Beginnings of Ulysses* (Michigan: UMI Research Press, 1983).

4 Arturo Schwarz, *Marcel Duchamp. Notes and Projects for the Large Glass* (London: Thames and Hudson, 1969) p. 1.

5 *Marcel Duchamp*, ed. P. Hulten (London: Thames and Hudson, 1993) pp. 17–18.

6 The phrase is Harry Levin's. Introduction, *James Joyce. Ulysses. A Facsimile of the Manuscript* (London: Faber, 1975) p. 11.

7 "Mr Bennet and Mrs Brown," in *The Captain's Death Bed and Other Essays* (New York: Harcourt, Brace & World Inc, 1950) p. 116.

8 Levin, p. 10.

9 In Schwarz, p. 7.

10 Hulten, 25/12/1949 & 30/9/1948, resp. (The biographical section of this book is organized as "Ephemerides," day to day installments set out in terms of the astrological calendar.)

11 Marcel Duchamp, "The Creative Act", in R. Lebel, *Marcel Duchamp* (New York: Grove Press, 1959) p. 78.

12 Hulten, 16/10/34.

13 Dorothy Dudley in Hulten, 3/11/34.

14 Hans Walter Gabler, *Ulysses: Critical and Synoptic Edition* (New York: Garland, 1982, vol. 3, p. 1895).

15 See Jerome McGann, "Ulysses as a Postmodern Text: The Gabler Edition," *Criticism*, Summer (1985) xxvii, 3, pp. 283–306, and Stephen Heath, "Ambiviolences: Notes for Reading Joyce," in D. Attridge & D. Ferrer, eds., *Post-Structuralist Joyce. Essays From the French* (Cambridge: Cambridge University Press, 1984) p. 39.

16 Frank Budgen, pp. 176–7.

17 *Letters*, Vol. 3, ed., R. Ellmann (London: Faber, 1975) pp. 30–1.

18 Dorothy Dudley in Hulten, 3/11/34.

19 *Ulysses* (London: Allen and Unwin, 1982) pp. 125 & 64 resp.

20 *The Pursuit of Signs: Semiotics, Literature, Deconstruction* (London: Routledge & Kegan Paul, 1981) p. 117.

21 See Stephen Heath, p. 32.

22 Marcel Duchamp, "Kind of Subtitle. Delay in Glass," *The Bride Stripped Bare by Her Bachelors, even. A Typographic Version*, by R. Hamilton, of Marcel Duchamp's *Green Box*, trans., G.H. Hamilton (Stuttgart: Edition Hansjorg Mayer, 1976) p. i.

23 Jacques Derrida, "Two Words For Joyce," in Attridge & Ferrer, p. 148.

24 *Letters*, Vol. 1, ed., S. Gilbert (London: Faber, 1957) p. 173.

25 "The Ulysses of James Joyce," *The Criterion*, 1, October (1922) p. 102.

26 Derrida, p. 148.

27 Myron Krueger, in M. Heim, *The Metaphysics of Virtual Reality* (Oxford: Oxford University Press, 1993) p. viii.

[7] *Ulysses* Returns

"Ulysses gives a great deal of trouble to everybody, not excluding myself," Joyce wrote to John Quinn in 1920, referring to the "world-troubling seaman" who had fired his imagination as a boy.[1] Joyce was no doubt reflecting, too, on the trouble that his *Ulysses* was causing for a literary world apparently unprepared for the daring and magnitude of his own tale of heroic return. Joyce's experiments with narrative technique, his treatment of point of view and manipulation of verbal texture challenged contemporary novelistic practice; his representation of the body and uninhibited display of sexuality outraged public morality as well as a number of his more influential supporters (Ezra Pound worried that urination was lascivious). Outrage, too, transformed typists into censors, and law suits hampered the novel's serialization in *The Little Review*, tempering the enthusiasm of prospective editors into wariness. In 1920 Joyce despaired of ever seeing his book in print; however, the turbulent prehistory of the publication of *Ulysses* in 1922 indicates that controversy, interference, mishap and misunderstanding would be the defining characteristics of its reception. Seventy-seven years later and eighteen editions down the line, the publication of *Ulysses* still preoccupies Joyce scholars, and contrary to Joyce's doleful vision in 1920, echoed by the autobiographical Stephen Dedalus ("Who ever anywhere will read these written words?") *Ulysses* won't be left alone.

Ulysses continues to fascinate new readers as a work of literature, which is no mean feat in the age of computerized, expanded books. Joyce realized the potential of the written word more than any other writer of this century (possibly of any century). At a time when the cultural technology of print is in transition, *Ulysses* is perhaps one of the few remaining products of literate culture that can be called auratic. We are still understanding its cultural impact, still catching up with its radical orchestration of what we have come to refer to as textuality. The book described in *Finnegans Wake* as

Ulysses, Shakespeare
and Company,
Paris, 1922.

ULYSSES

by

JAMES JOYCE

SHAKESPEARE AND COMPANY

12, Rue de l'Odéon, 12

PARIS

1922

being "usylessly unreadable" sustains a lively and varied reading public, in part because it has transcended the critical agendas of modernism and has anticipated those of postmodernism, in the process resisting the attempts of exegetes determined to exhaust it of meaning. *Ulysses* sustains its resonance as a labyrinth, promising infuriation and exhilaration. Perhaps a more significant explanation of its endurance lies in the conspicuous attraction it has generated for over seventy years as a work in progress. *Ulysses*, it seems, is the great unfinished monument of modernism.

The first publication of *Ulysses* in 1922 has proven to be a commencement rather than a conclusion, and since that time the book has been haunted (like Stephen) by the specter of corruption, in the form of "numerous typographical errors unavoidable under the exceptional circumstances" — a disclaimer that was not only a great under-statement, but the book's formal registration that further work was required. Prior to Hans Walter Gabler's "definitive" critical and synoptic edition of 1984, the various attempts to correct the text between 1922 and 1961 (the last time the book had been corrected and reset) only served to reinforce its unfinished status, for in the process of restoration, correction and emendation, new errors, both typographical and editorial, crept in unnoticed. The possibility of establishing a definitive text preoccupied Joyceans during the 1960s, especially in Jack Dalton's singlehanded attempts to cor-rect the 1961 Random House edition. In 1973 a committee was established to clean up the "Blue Book of Eccles," and over a decade later, Gabler's claim to have corrected seven errors per page (5,000 in all) and in the process restored "*Ulysses* as Joyce wrote it," confirmed for many of the big names in Joyce scholarship that it could at last be claimed (as Joyce had said to Valéry Larbaud and Robert McAlmon in October 1921) that *Ulysses* was finished. To emphasize this act of finality, Hugh Kenner celebrated the eventual completion of the drawn out publication of the book by suggesting the extension of its famous endline "Trieste-Zurich-Paris, 1914-1922" to include "Char-lottesville-Philadelphia-Buffalo-Cambridge-Austin-London-Munich, 1977-1984."[2]

Gabler's "computerized" *Ulysses*, as it came to be known, didn't enjoy its claim to fame for very long. After the initial celebration of its publication on Bloomsday 1984, critics set about evaluating this *Ulysses* as it had never been seen before, and some of them didn't like what they saw. Suspicion about editorial procedure soon turned to scepticism and condemnation. The private research of critics who had made it their business to devote emergent careers as Joyceans to the deconstruction of the "new" *Ulysses* very quickly became public debate on the international Joyce circuit at confer-ences devoted exclusively to assessing the Gabler edition, in the rarefied circles of tex-tual scholarship, and in the pages of the *Times Literary Supplement*. The most prominent of Gabler's critics was John Kidd, a self-styled Joycean vigilante from the University of Virginia, who sold his private library to fund research expeditions to uni-versities that held manuscripts and other archival material relevant to his cause. Kidd, then a research fellow, boldly argued that Gabler's *Ulysses* was far from accurate, and that as a result of a misguided and irresponsible working notion of what constituted Joyce's copytext, he had contributed to rather than corrected the errors of previous editions.

It had not gone unnoticed that this controversy was taking place at a time when the copyright on *Ulysses* was due to expire, and that it would soon be in the pubic domain. Gabler's text was given the nod by the Joyce Estate as a new, standard edition, amid growing concern that the implications of Kidd's criticism had not been fully explored, or satisfactorily countered by Gabler and his editorial team, and the committee of scholars responsible for advising the Joyce Estate. Allegations of imposture, of shoddy editing and unjustified claims followed the publication in 1986 of the first and only trade edition of the "*Corrected Ulysses*." In June 1988 Kidd published his inflammatory denunciation of Gabler's text, "The Scandal of 'Ulysses,'" and for a year an internecine battle of charge and countercharge between Kidd and Gabler and their respective supporters was waged in the pages of the *New York Review of Books*. One of the more startling revelations to emerge was an ongoing, and it goes without saying, concealed dissent among Gabler and his team of assistants and academic advisors. Kidd, it seems, was a latecomer to criticism of Gabler's editorial procedure. As with most slinging matches of this kind, the salient issues were soon forgotten, as the debate deteriorated into trivia, repetition and abuse.

Just as the debate surrounding the Gabler edition looked like going on indefinitely, so too did the relentless project of finishing Joyce's "*edition de tenebres*." But the suggestion that Gabler would continue making corrections and amendments to successive printings of the 1986 trade edition clearly evidenced that the belief in a definitive *Ulysses* as Joyce wrote it was the very factor responsible for the endemic corruption that everyone, including Joyce himself, had attempted in vain to clean up since 1922. As Clive Hart noted in 1984, "the perfect *Ulysses*, totally harmonious, entirely error-free, the *Ulysses* that has never existed, can never exist."[3] The unrelenting pursuit of unequivocal authority had blinded Gabler and his associates to the simple reality that Joyce's composition of *Ulysses* made it impossible ("virtually" so, too, given that he placed so much store in the technology of simulation) to determine a unified autograph. First, there was no complete manuscript to stand as copytext, and Joyce was still making changes to proof as the book was being printed (up until two days before it was published, in fact). Secondly, revision and correction of transmissional documents was responsible for a third of the text published in 1922. Working from memory, Joyce notoriously made different corrections on two, and sometimes three sets of typescript and proof, so on this basis it is reasonable to assert that any such inscription is authorial; as he noted himself in *Finnegans Wake*, "every splurge on the vellum he blundered over was an aisling vision more gorgeous than the one before." What then emerges as Joyce's autograph text is a shifting, decentered creative space in which substitution and differentiation flicker, inviting readerly negotiation of textual options. To think of *Ulysses* in this way, as a discontinuous, multi-layered holograph, is to assign Joyce an immortality the likes of which he could not have anticipated. It has been suggested that Joyce's accretive method of composition meant that he never actually finished writing *Ulysses*, and that publication marked a pause, a caesura in the creative process where he was prepared to let a version stand for public scrutiny — the 1922 *Ulysses*, then, was merely one version of an indeterminate number of potential combinations of Joyce's compositional process.

Gabler's contentious decision to pass over the 1922 Shakespeare and Co. edition as a copytext, and instead reconstruct its antecedent process of composition, reveals the futility and presumption of the task he set himself. The genetic or "continuous manuscript text" Gabler purported to re-create was constituted not only of available manuscript and archival material, but required the intervention of editorial judgements based on hypothetical and lost manuscripts. But there are also intricate unknowables to be taken into account, such as verbal instructions to typists or the printer of which there are no record or which were written down but are now lost. Similarly, the vast majority of the 5,000 changes made by Gabler were accidentals (the irony of the term, under the circumstances, would have not been lost on anyone acquainted with the history of *Ulysses*), and in the process of correcting the errors of wayward typists and displacements in the typesetting, Gabler corrected intentional misspellings and Anglicized Gaelic names. The confusion over authorial intention was best represented in the restored fragment of Stephen's interior monologue in which he nominates love as the elusive "word known to all men." In recovering this momentous definition, the loss of which had been attributed to a typist's eyeskip, Gabler had helped solve the riddle of "Scylla and Charybdis" (the episode in which it is located). The critical excitement surrounding this crucial link in a cross-referential chain that had kept the professors busy for some time hardly seemed worth the effort, for two reasons. First, certain critics had already surmised that "the big word" in *Ulysses* was in fact love (most notably, Richard Ellmann, in *Ulysses on the Liffey*, 1972). Suffering from a guilty conscience for not having prayed at his mother's deathbed, Stephen broods at length on "love's bitter mystery," and while he reflects (with no little irony) that it is "Love that dare not speak its name," it is enough of a theme to unite him with Bloom, who does name it, in the face of adversity. It is while confronted with the apparition of his reproachful mother, in the "Nighttown" episode, that Stephen, too, wants to hear it named. Secondly, the celebrated recovery was such a perfect instance of the indeterminacy and incertitude that so often beguiles textual editors that any claims of authorial approval to support its inclusion had little value, or indeed authority, outside the opinions of Gabler as an editor. The missing passage had in fact been available since 1975, in a limited edition facsimile of the Rosenbach facsimile, the set of fair copies written out by Joyce between 1917 and 1921. As Bruce Arnold indicated in *The Scandal of Ulysses. The Sensational Life of A Twentieth-Century Masterpiece* (1991), his comprehensive study of the history of *Ulysses* publishing, the issue of the existence of the passage was hardly momentous, or even contentious, as it was well known to scholars from the Rosenbach manuscript. The real issue concerned inclusion, of "whether or not it should be put it in."[4] Speculation of this sort is treacherous. If the recovered passage was so thematically central as has been claimed, it would be reasonable to expect Joyce to have picked it up and incorporated it into any one of the reprints he worked on between 1922 and 1924. Joyce's meticulous weaving of patterns and motifs attests to his cognizance of detail, and if he can chase a potato in Bloom's pocket throughout the entire book, the pursuit of lost love was surely weighty enough to occupy his attentions. On the other hand, Joyce was notorious for textual play, and setting traps for the unwary reader seems to have been a particular delight. Joyce may well have been aware of the original omission and saw that it was good. We can conjecture and project a scenario of Joycean textual aporia, but when it comes down to it, we will never know. In matters such as these, we will just have to accept that our knowledge is, unavoidably, like the home without Plumtree's potted meat.

This is the story of Pierre Menard re-told: re-write "the" *Ulysses* by simulating the creative mind of Joyce. The principle of prudent, considered deduction of what Joyce intended over his own variations and those of a third party (which was essential to Gabler's editorial theory), is actually closer to the process of abductive reasoning (in Peirce's sense of the term), for editorial judgment under these circumstances involves a degree of risk-taking and relies upon the cohesion and plausibility of a judgment within the formation of a possible compositional scenario rather than indisputable authenticity. Gabler indirectly acknowledged this in his afterword to the 1986 Student Edition of the much maligned "corrected text," noting that no "text written or edited can be wholly divorced from the processes of writing and editing and the decisions and judgments that they entail. Hence, definitive texts do not in truth exist, but at the most approximations to the best possible text."[5] Gabler would have perhaps been better off simply presenting a textual apparatus that attempted to map the complex genesis of the compositional process (his "synoptic text") and to critically compare variant readings, leaving his reader to negotiate what might be Joyce from scribe, compositor or eyeskip. Gabler made the mistake of believing that the judgments he made on the basis of available data recovered what had been elusive to Joyce himself. Deirdre Bair made the same mistake when she thought that reading Samuel Beckett's letters to Thomas McGreevy in the light of his writing was the aperçu to her subject's psyche. A critical edition of the Beckett/McGreevy letters would have been a major contribution to Beckett scholarship. Her biography was not.

If we have learned anything from the controversial history of the attempts of editors to write the text that Joyce wanted to write, it is simply that any edition of *Ulysses* is irreducible to any master, or even ideal text. It is appropriate to think of the complex field of inscriptions that constitutes the multi-textuality of *Ulysses* as a palimpsest, and while the decentred act of its creation is illegible, its traces abound. History, too, has shown that the Gabler experiment could not sustain its much publicized monopoly, and in 1990 Random House reissued its 1961 imprint. Penguin followed suit in 1992, noting in a spirit of Joycean atonement that "this edition returns to the standard Random House/Bodley Head text that first appeared in 1960," the text, according to Kidd, that is apparently closest to *Ulysses* as Joyce last saw it. The 1922 text is closer again, and as the strange logic of return that circulates throughout *Ulysses* and its publishing act would have it, this very edition was reissued in paperback by Oxford University Press in 1993. As the "new" *Ulysses* lost its appeal, the mystique and historical resonance of the "old" one has revived acceptance of the 1922 *Ulysses* as a flawed masterpiece, for which no substitute will do ("First choice for the original Joyce," declares an OUP advertisement for the book). This edition, though, is highly self-conscious of the entire publishing controversy, from Joyce's time to the present, and as the introduction and appendices attest, the text is circumscribed by the contours of more recent debates that have inevitably established the pretext for just such an edition. Oxford's promotional literature emphasizes that this edition is the only one to reproduce the 1922 text, and it proudly does so "without interference," which is not quite true, for, as its editor Jeri Johnson points out, the worst instances of typographical corruption have been emended "for the sake of readability."[6] Despite the inclusion of a meticulous comparative listing of the errata sheets appended to reprints of *Ulysses* in Joyce's lifetime, no indication is given of what corrections have been made for this edition, or the rationale behind them, which is highly problematic, for as a glance at the errata lists will reveal, knowing what is Joyce from what is not requires discrimination between "hides and hints and misses in prints."

Jeri Johnson, the editor of this 1922 *Ulysses*, points out that the 1922 edition has only previously been commercially available in reduced facsimile, as part of the limited edition Rosenbach Manuscript collection of 1975. While we are not strictly getting the 1922 edition arts and wall, we are possibly getting something closer to it than has ever been available before as a trade edition. There is something attractive about a trade edition of the 1922 *Ulysses*, for most people these days have only ever read about it, or relished its presence in the rare book rooms of state or university libraries. The composition, publication and reception of the 1922 text is part of twentieth century cultural lore, and the Oxford reissue, edited as it is, will no doubt reinforce its significance as a literary *unicum*.

And so after all the "alphybettyformed verbage" surrounding the desirability of a standardized *Ulysses*, there are at least two to choose from since the 1986 Gabler text fell from grace (in the United States copyright restrictions mean that the 1961 Random House and Gabler editions are the only ones available). This is probably the most desirable situation to have emerged from the scandals of *Ulysses*, and it is consistent with the fate of Joyce's contemporary Proust, for whom three separate editions of *A La Recherche du Temps Perdu* have appeared since his work became public domain in 1987. Editors of Proust, too, had considered for some time that an ideal text is theoretically possible, but practically unfeasible, since the danger of an "infinite regress of reading" into early drafts and the like means that one may enter the textual traces of Proust's workshop, but, as Roger Shattuck and Douglas Alden have observed, determining what Proust would have used from "the ruins" is not a decision for editors to make.[7]

*

The laws of cyclic return are implacable, as Joyce knew only too well. However, when the *Sporting Times* (the "Pink 'Un") coined its famous broadside "The Scandal of *Ulysses*" in 1922, no one, probably not even Joyce, who aspired to the condition of immortality, could have anticipated that such a catchcry would still have currency on the eve of the new millennium. *Ulysses* is no longer scandalous in moral terms, though scandal, in a more general sense, is the particular "flavour" of the book's original publication that has been generated by its most recent editor. In 1997 Picador published Danis Rose's "Reader's Edition" of *Ulysses* to immediate cries of protestation from the James Joyce Estate, academics, antiquarian booksellers and, unfortunately for Rose, readers. Part of the problem was that Rose didn't conceive himself as just any other editor. Literally applying Jerome McGann's collaborative model of book production, which identifies the author and the creative act as part of a much larger cultural and institutional praxis, Rose positioned himself as a latter-day publisher, offering the reading public, for the first time, "*Ulysses* as James Joyce wrote it." Following McGann's analysis of "how books are actually produced," Rose worked from the principle that the editor "should replace the original production crew when copyreading." Furthermore, "the edition's publisher's typographers and designers" (under the direction and discretion of the editor) "should replace their original counterparts."[8] The relationship between Rose's sense of what James Joyce actually wrote over what he did not, or indeed should not have written, is thus at the center of this latest scandal of *Ulysses*.

Rose's "people's" *Ulysses* was predicated on a series of assumptions to do with who Joyce's readers were, how they conceived the act of reading, and how they felt about reading James Joyce's *Ulysses*. Rose, a Joyce scholar, started from the very anti-Joycean position that the "unpalatable" truth about *Ulysses* is that few readers get beyond the opening episodes and that most give up in despair.

Rose proclaimed himself as apologist for the common reader; that is, the reader who reads for pleasure, as distinct from the reader of Joyce, for whom reading is an agon. Concealed within his revolt against academic control of *Ulysses*, from the textual and interpretive point of view, was an assumption that *Ulysses*, as Joyce wrote it, was unreadable and did not afford the reader any pleasure. In 1997 Danis Rose dramatically arrived on the scene as the pander of pleasure, guaranteeing, through a prophylactic approach to difficult writing, to "maximise the pleasure of the reader." With Danis Rose you got to see everything with complete clarity. Indeed, Rose's definition of his isotext was suggestive, "an error-free, 'naked' transcription of the author's words" (xii) (ironic self-awareness won't do here, for as all, well most, Joyceans know, Joyce abhorred the use of "perverted commas"). Rose's sexualized *Ulysses*-experience clearly had more in common with the original scandal of *Ulysses* than at first appeared to be the case.

Many readers of *Ulysses* refused his services. One of the more vocal and recriminatory was John Kidd. Rose's credentials left him vulnerable to attack from the man who had assassinated Hans Walter Gabler in the 1980s. For Kidd, writing in the *New York Review of Books*, the *de fac*to theater of Joycean scandal, Rose's *Ulysses* was merely one in a line of "ill-starred" projects. A protégé of Gabler's, Rose immediately carried the stain of ignominy. He had also, Kidd informed us with relish, been dismissed as editor of an Estate edition of *Finnegans Wake*. Kidd's criticism of Rose was ostensibly the same as that meted out to Gabler a decade earlier, especially the charges that many of his changes were made with no reference to manuscripts or transmissional documents.[9] Kidd asserted that like Gabler, Rose hadn't turned up any new manuscript evidence to support his interventionist practices nor had he checked facsimiles against originals for discrimination between printer's and authorial marks (unlike Gabler's variorum edition of 1984, there was no textual apparatus published in the "Reader's" edition, and its absence will mean that the pandy bat will be routinely applied with Father Dolan's vigour). The lack of a critical apparatus to substantiate his

71

editorial decisions or justify his preferences for actual changes to Joyce's text, made it virtually impossible to secure any credibility for the edition, especially in the coteries of textual editing. Without any genetic documents to appeal to, Rose made decisions concerning authorial intention or authorial error on the tenuous assumption that a mistake is the only logical explanation when "a sentence is saying something it should not – where the logic of the narrative is inexplicably broken." (xvii) Since so much of the poetry of *Ulysses* falls into this category, especially the characters' interior monologues, it's a wonder more of the text hasn't been tampered with. How did the following escape Rose's Oedipal eye: "Perfume of embraces all him assailed. With hungered flesh obscurely, he mutely craved to adore." Perhaps something like this would have been more in keeping with his practice and concern for easy intelligibility: "Perfume of embraces assailed him. Obscurely, with hungering flesh, he craved to adore" (the second adverb removed because it was superfluous and added nothing to the sense). Robin Bates, writing of the Gabler/Kidd dispute in 1990, unwittingly summed up, in advance, what has become the standard critical response to the Rose style-sheet for textual faults: "Most assuredly what I *don't* want is a version of *Ulysses* by some expert who thinks he knows better than Joyce."[10]

Many of the changes Rose made in the interests of "greater ease" were based on a far from convincing assertion that any sustained reading of *Ulysses* was difficult because of a "gradual accumulation of irritations," such as "simple errors, eccentric and wrong spelling, flawed punctuation, excessive use of compounds." Given Rose's temperance in the face of Joycean excess, how was "Wavewhite wedded words" allowed to stand (Maurice Darantiere's Dijon compositors ran out of w's during the printing of the 1922 edition)? Rose also made alterations to typographical features of the text, of which Joyce was quite specific, if idiosyncratic, making, for example, the banner headlines or captions much smaller and less obtrusive in "Aeolus." Rose corrected the famous unpunctuated Molly Bloom soliloquy, his rationale being that their absence is irritating. Punctuation, argued Rose, was necessary for the comprehension of the words, and since "readers of *Ulysses* are compelled mentally to resupply" them anyway, "nothing really has been gained by their removal and a great deal – the undisturbed flow of the text – has been lost." (xxv) Overall, then, Rose's response was to simplify, to smooth out Joyce's troublesome roughness and thereby return *Ulysses* to the people as an easy read. His strategy, when applied to Joycean wordplay: hyphenate. It seems that late twentieth century readers have lost the ability to make sense of compound words as well as the tolerance for linguistic experimentation of Joyce's contemporary audience. Beyond the questionable logic that hyphenating compound words heightens the reader's pleasure of the text (editors of Lewis Carroll have yet to cotton on to this), Rose is beguilingly inconsistent in his practice; in the first episode "snotgreen" is made more pleasurable ("snot-green"), while in the very next sentence "scrotumtightening" is passed over. The same occurs with "wave-white" and "wavenoise;" while "heaventree" stands, while "night-blue" is clearly too diffi-cult for words.

Notwithstanding Rose's spurious assumption that lovers of literature value simplic-ity, and that a user-friendly *Ulysses* will help more people finish reading it, his conspic-uous and unfathomable inconsistency in matters such as hyphenation discredits his self-portrait as a craftsman tidying up aesthetic misjudgments made by the book's author, who, in the lexicon of Rose's editorial practice, was guilty of "textual faults." (xvii) It's hardly surprising that Rose's critics, and there were many of them, accused him of self-aggrandisement, editorial capriciousness and philistinism; one writer not-ing that Rose's presumptuous notion of a user-friendly *Ulysses* makes the text look like "anything else we find at an airport." Criticism very quickly descended into parody, Rose being stereotyped as a manic user of hyphenation, with jokes of the "or should that be hyphen-ation" type being *de rigueur*. When parody was not the prevailing mode, indignant hostility was. Lawrence Rainey, writing in the *London Review of Books* (pre-dating Kidd's attack by several months), asserted that Rose's edition rep-resented "the reign of an editorial theory which violates every principle and procedure of critical editing, replacing it with nothing more than 'making sense' as construed, tautologically, by Danis Rose."[11]

One of the more notable contributions to the ongoing hustle of charge and counter-charge in trans-Atlantic literary broadsheets was Stephen James Joyce's letter to the *Times Literary Supplement*. The celebrated grandson of the now putative author of *Ulysses* demanded that if the Rose edition was to remain on the market, then "the name of James Joyce must be eliminated, stricken from the dust-jacket, cover and inside title-pages of this edition." Not satisfied with charges of "outrageous misrepre-sentation," Joyce asserted that the literary world had gone beyond the scandal of *Ulysses*, entreating, "is this not 'The Rape of *Ulysses*'?!"[12]

The scandals of Danis Rose suggest that *Ulysses* has at least moved beyond the "Kidd Era." Suggestion can be deceptive. John Kidd had made such a public nuisance of himself since his 1985 sortie "Errors of Execution in the 1984 *Ulysses*" that his influ-ence just won't go away. A 1997 feature story in the journal *Lingua Franca* dubbed him "the corrections officer."[13] The piece, written by Robin Bates, was very pro-Kidd, por-traying him as an editorial terrier, running down every proper name and missing caret.

But "the corrections officer," with its suggestions of cocksure pedantry, was a term of derision, rather than endearment, for many in the Joyce world. While the story portrayed Kidd as something of an authority on editing *Ulysses*, it did little to counteract the perception that for all his *sturm und drang* as an antagonist of Gabler and Rose, he had produced virtually nothing in the way of a superior text that could stand peer review and criticism. Squabbles over publication rights between Norton, Kidd's publisher, and Random House, had purportedly becalmed the completion of his print edition (according to Kidd and his proponents). However by July 1998, when Boston University discontinued funding Kidd's James Joyce Research Center, it was not exactly clear how near to completion Kidd's edition was. Most of his critics argued that it was far from complete, and was unlikely to receive further sponsorship. This also meant the suspension of work on his *Annotated Ulysses on CD-ROM*, on which he had been working for years, since the 1922 edition he had been preparing for publication with Norton was to be the basis of that project. History will probably show that bravado, not bravura, would mark the end of the Kidd era.

There can be no final word when it comes to the problematics of *Ulysses* and textual editing. Despite the recommendations of critical heavyweights such as the late Anthony Burgess to "leave it alone,"[14] there will only ever be continuities, new developments, new debates, as long as the book is in print or electronic form. Work continues apace on what will be the first full hypermedia edition of *Ulysses*, under the direction of Michael Groden, a Joycean with an impressive track record of scholarly and archival work on *Ulysses*. Unlike Kidd's aborted *Annotated Ulysses on CD-ROM*, Groden's hypermedia *Ulysses* project is supported by an impressive infrastructure of the most respected writers and scholars in the Joyce industry, among them Hugh Kenner, Fritz Senn, and Clive Hart. Groden has taken the canny decision to include a range of editions, including the 1922 first edition, subsequent editions published in Joyce's lifetime and the Gabler edition. This multi-textual, hyperlinked *Ulysses* will be highly useful for research purposes, enabling the comparison of different editions, the scansion of variants, and importantly, offering individual researchers the opportunity to make their own decisions concerning the ring of rightness of a word or a cadence. The inclusion of multimedia, such as images and maps of Dublin in 1904, audio-visual ephemera (pronunciation of proper names, sampling of relevant sound) and video, will make this edition of *Ulysses* the first to include a comprehensive archive of the kinds of para-cultural material that scholars and avid readers alike seek out to enhance their experience of the text as a multisensory epiphenomenon. Detailed scholarly annotations for each of the eighteen episodes, as well as critical essays and commentaries, will extend this expanded *Ulysses* even further, providing the closest thing in Joyce criticism to an integrated *Ulysses* network.

The coming age of electronic Joyce will not be exempt from the scandals of *Ulysses*. The very notion of a hypertextual *Ulysses* will be anathema for many readers of Joyce, for whom the printed book and its associated habits of reading have secured safe passage for its hero. A networked *Ulysses* carries the promise, but also the threat, of an ongoing journey, endless wanderings through a web of interlinked editions. But perhaps there will also be a familiar narrative dimension to a networked *Ulysses*. Hypertextuality, by its very nature, is aberrant; journeys begun are soon stymied by the agon of choice, of the unavoidable necessity to encounter distraction. The pursuit of a singular goal or final outcome is drawn out, multiplied, nested as a labyrinth of goals within goals. As obstacles are defeated, the trials and tribulations of getting back on course become tasks in themselves, an ongoing process of striving and overcoming. In dramatizing this sense of an ending, the achievement of Ithaca becomes more clear than ever as the occasion for the journey.

1 James Joyce letter to John Quinn, 17 November, 1920, New York Public Library, Manuscripts Division.
2 Hugh Kenner, "Leopold's Bloom Restored," *The Times Literary Supplement*, 13 July (1984) p. 771.
3 Clive Hart, "Art Thou Real, My Ideal?" in C. George Sandulescu and Clive Hart, eds. *Assessing the 1984 "Ulysses"* (New Jersey: Barnes & Noble, 1986) p. 65.
4 Bruce Arnold, *The Scandal of Ulysses. The Sensational Life of a Twentieth-Century Masterpiece* (New York: St. Martin's Press, 1991) p. 149.
5 Hans Walter Gabler, Afterword, *Ulysses. The Corrected Text* (Student's Edition) (Harmondsworth: Penguin, 1986) p. 650.
6 *Ulysses*, ed. Jeri Johnson (Oxford: Oxford University Press, 1993) p. lvi.
7 Roger Shattuck and Douglas Alden, "Searching for the True Text," *The Times Literary Supplement*, June10-16 (1988) p. 641.
8 *Ulysses. A Reader's Edition*, ed. Danis Rose (London: Picador, 1997) p. xv. Further references to this edition are given after quotations in the text.
9 John Kidd, "Making the Wrong Joyce," *The New York Review of Books*, XLIV, 14, September 25 (1997) p. 54.
10 Robin Bates, "Reflections on the Kidd Era," *Studies in the Novel* (A Special Issue on Editing *Ulysses*), ed. Charles Rossman, xxii, 2, Summer (1990) p. 130.
11 Lawrence Rainey, "How Molly Bloom Got Her Apostrophes," *London Review of Books*, 19, 12, 19 June (1997) p. 13.
12 Stephen James Joyce, "The 'Reader's edition' of *Ulysses*," *The Times Literary Supplement*, 27 June (1997) p. 17.
13 Robin Bates, "The Corrections Officer," *Lingua Franca*, October (1997).
14 Anthony Burgess, quoted in Arnold, p. 246.

[8] Samuel Beckett, Francis Bacon and the Ferocious Dilemma of Expression

Within literature and painting, the work of Samuel Beckett and Francis Bacon has been identified as this century's most graphic portrayal of what Bacon, in a resonant phrase, called "the brutality of fact." Beckett's gallery of moribunds and abjects are readily called to mind in the claustrophobic, excrescential imagery of Bacon, and critics have persistently drawn parallels between their representations of the violence and futility of *la condition humaine*. In his 1993 biography of Francis Bacon, Andrew Sinclair attempted to redress this thematic stereotyping, noting that with Beckett, Bacon "spoke for a very intense life, not for a belief in death or horror. Their human figures were unconquerable. They endured by their insistence and their presence, even when threatened by mutilation or failure or fall."[1] Describing both of them as artists "of endgame,"[2] Sinclair emphasizes the emotional pitch of their work. However, the term also draws attention to the problematic status of the creative act itself in their work. To end, to enact a decisive completion of the creative process was for both of them an important preoccupation, both artistically and critically. This preoccupation involves the persistence of a dialectic between what I will call pictorial time and critical space. In both cases the most sustained discussion of the aesthetics responsible for a conception of pictorial time is to be found in interviews rather than explicit manifestos. David Sylvester's *The Brutality of Fact. Interviews with Francis Bacon* is a fairly conventional document, involving an interviewer talking to a recognized painter in a series of interviews recorded between 1962 and 1986. They are conversational and informative, organized around standard themes: biographical detail, artistic development, technique, art history and genealogy. Samuel Beckett's *Three Dialogues with Georges Duthuit*, conducted over a number of days in 1948 and written up later by Beckett from memory, focuses quite specifically on three modern painters: Pierre Tal Coat, André Masson and Bram van Velde, and is much narrower in its range (the dialogues were originally published by Duthuit a year later in *transition*). Beckett and Duthuit are adversaries, intellectual sparring partners rather than interviewer and subject, and the mood of the discussion is intense and self-consciously precocious; a feature attributable, reputedly, to augmentation in the writing rather than a characteristic of the actual proceedings.

Despite these differences, though, these interviews are united by a revolutionary vision, a theory of painting as an inexpressive, intransitive act. Both Bacon and Beckett are interested in the process of painting as an end in itself, and both espouse the radical view that the finished product, the art object, is dispensable, both in practice and within critical discourse. Beckett, as Vivian Mercier has noted, fails to discuss a single work of art throughout the course of the Duthuit dialogues. Any references made to the material fact of the canvas are simply to invoke the abjection of their creation, as he noted of the work of Masson:

> Though little familiar with the problems he has set himself in the past and which, by the mere fact of their solubility or for any other reason, have lost for him their legitimacy, I feel their presence not far behind these canvases veiled in consternation, and the scars of a competence that must be most painful to him.[3]

Throughout his career, Bacon destroyed many of his paintings, recognizing in them a failure to embody the process that went into their making, what Sylvester calls the "residue of the activity"[4] (if representatives of Marlborough Fine Art had not made a habit of removing his canvases, still wet, from his studio, many more would have been lost). For Bacon self-expression in painting is banal, for in relying on what can be done "with ease," (91) the making of a statement fails to confront the task of making, of "making like," in the first place:

> There are standards set up as to what appearance is or should be, but there's no doubt that the ways appearance can be made are very mysterious ways, because one knows that by some accidental brushmarks suddenly appearance comes in with a vividness that no accepted way of doing it would have brought about. (105)

There is a remarkable similarity in their respective endorsement of the need to rid painting of traditional narrative and expressive significations, to produce the pictorial equivalent of *écriture*, in Roland Barthes' sense of zero degree writing. For Bacon, the violent distortion of appearance is necessary to "break the willed articulation of the image," (160) for in the age of photography and mechanical reproduction, painting has had to re-define its function in relation to appearance ("the whole questioning of what appearance is," (105)). Beckett is interested in total departure from "the plane of the feasible," (103) a disgusted turning away from representation of any recognizable or logical kind; he avows an art "weary of puny exploits, weary of pretending to be able, of being able, of doing a little better the same old thing." (103) It is in the painting of Bram Van Velde that Beckett identifies an "art of a different order," (119) which, *vis á vis* the history of painting, has submit itself "wholly to the incoercible absence of relation." (125)

Beckett refers to Masson as being "literally skewered on the ferocious dilemma of expression." (110) This is the most fitting, descriptive image of the concept of the creative act which Bacon and Beckett share (the degree of conceptual overlap between them is considerable, and phrases of Beckett's are consistently descriptive of Bacon, and vice versa). The creative act, for both of them, is defined in terms of indigence, failure and ignorance. Bacon frequently comments on his impotence in the face of how to do what he might want to do. The conventional methods of figuration are too far removed from what he calls the "emanation" of his subject, particularly in his portraits. His desire to "deform people into appearance" (146) signals not only his aesthetic project of returning both himself and the spectator of his work to life "more violently," (141) but his perception of the unavoidable necessity of chance and accident as fundamental characteristics of the act of composition ("what really happens comes about in working" (149)). Opposing narrative and "illustrational paint," Bacon refers to "non-rational marks," (58) and for him the "mystery of fact" (58) is only capable of being captured in those aleatory moments when paint is "irrationally" applied to the canvas. It is the nervous system, rather than the mind, from which Bacon sees his images emanating, and to which he hopes they appeal.

For Beckett, Tal Coat, Masson and Van Velde have in varying degrees attempted to go beyond "the field of the possible." (103) Without stating it as such, Beckett intimates that the quest of the modern painter involves nothing less than a re-definition of the underlying assumptions of Western art, namely, "the common anxiety to express as much as possible, or as truly as possible, or as finely as possible, to the best of one's ability." (120) Tal Coat and Masson barely scratch the surface of what Beckett calls an "art of a different order." Bram van Velde is the "first to accept a certain situation and to consent to a certain act:" (119)

> Others have felt that art is not necessarily expression. But the numerous attempts made to make painting independent of its occasion have only succeeded in enlarging its repertory. I suggest that van Velde is the first whose painting is bereft, rid if you prefer, of occasion in every shape and form, ideal as well as material, and the first whose hands have not been tied by the certitude that expression is an impossible act. (121)

While Bacon recognizes the centrality of the problem of making in the compositional process, he is still concerned with the production of an image. He concedes, regretfully, that "in spite of theoretically longing for the image to be made up of irrational marks, inevitably illustration has to come into it..." (126) Bacon is acutely aware that the fundamental problem for him is that in working with likeness, with appearance, he is unavoidably working with illustrational marks. In his portraits, then, he faces the paradoxical situation of wanting, through distortion of the appearance, to evade illustration, and yet retain a defamiliarized re-making of the image of the sitter, producing what Gilles Deleuze has called "the figural."[5] However, it is the apparent insuperability of this situation that constitutes the painterly act for Bacon. The difficulty of figuration and the refusal to resort to abstraction is the tension, the self-imposed difficulty which ensures that "the mystery of appearance" remains indistinguishable from "the mystery of the making." (105) Beckett also characterizes the act of painting in terms of a search for difficulty. The "malady of wanting to know what to do and the malady of wanting to be able to do it" (110) results in the condition of oppression which Beckett identifies as the defining characteristic of his art of a different order. Beckett, too, is aware that "anything and everything is doomed to become occasion, including... the pursuit of occasion." (124) However Beckett is more extreme than Bacon, more agonistic in his understanding of the creative act, in that he eschews any object of painting other than the unidentified compulsion to paint, as outlined in his infamous mantra:

> The expression that there is nothing to express, nothing with which to express, nothing from which to express, no power to express, no desire to express, together with the obligation to express. (103)

Beckett professes a painterly act bereft of occasion, free of any kind of image, but at the same time acknowledges that the plane he seeks is logically unavailable to the painter. Both Bacon and Beckett acknowledge the frustration of the predicament they face in proposing an art that is theoretically audacious, yet impossible in practice. In the words of Bacon:

> I think that in our previous discussions, when we've talked about the possibility of making appearance out of something which was not illustration, I've over-talked about it. Because, in spite of theoretically longing for the image to be made up of irrational marks, inevitably illustration has to come into it to make certain parts of the head and face which, if one left them out, one would then only be making an abstract design. I think what I very often have talked about has been perhaps a particular theory of mine which is impossible to achieve. (126)

This is one of the few instances in the published interviews with David Sylvester where Bacon openly admits to the futility of his aesthetic. It is interesting, too, that Bacon makes this disclosure without any prompting from Sylvester. Indeed, the exchange between Bacon and Sylvester throughout the interviews is generally uncontentious, and Sylvester frequently corroborates or expands upon Bacon's assertions in an effort to clarify and substantiate, rather than challenge or question them:

> **DS** Could one put it like this? – that you're trying to make an image of appearance that is conditioned as little as possible by the accepted standards of what appearance is.

> **FB** That's a very good way of putting it. There's a further step to that: the whole questioning of what appearance is. (105)

Beckett, on the other hand, has to struggle, and is hard pressed to uphold his views in the face of Duthuit's astute argument that "the occasion of (van Velde's) painting is his predicament, and that it is expressive of the impossibility to express?" Duthuit is, at times, quite the antagonist:

> **D** — Speaking of Tal Coat and Masson you invoked an art of a different order, not only from theirs, but from any achieved up to date. Am I right in thinking you had van Velde in mind when making this sweeping distinction?

> **B** — Yes. I think he is the first to accept a certain situation and to consent to a certain act.

> **D** — Would it be too much to ask you to state again, as simply as possible, the situation and act that you conceive to be his? (119)

The Beckett/Duthuit dialogues are more Platonic and dialectical than the Sylvester interviews with Bacon. This partly accounts for the obvious difference between two texts that are otherwise very similar in their aesthetic premises. The Bacon interviews proceed as an integrated discourse that theorizes an anti-representational art, the problems of achieving it, the potential response, or desired response of the spectator, even the notion that such art is "impervious to interpretation." (179) Bacon refers at one point to the hopelessness of talking about painting, since "one never does anything but talk around it." (100) However, Bacon makes no mention of the fact that his theory of art perhaps requires a different order of discourse, or, at least, places tremendous strain upon conventional discussions "around" art (of which his interviews with Sylvester are an example). Moreover, he seems to be naively unaware of the potential of his own aesthetic theory to disrupt and occasion a quite radical revision of critical discourse. The Duthuit dialogues are another matter. While the task of interpretation is not discussed, or is even specifically elicited as an issue, the implications of Beckett's theory for critical discourse, for "talking around" painting, are felt throughout the three dialogues. Duthuit's response to Beckett's cabala of the inexpressive is the assertion that it "is a violently extreme and personal point of view, of no help to us in the matter of Tal Coat." (103) Duthuit is frequently irascible in this way, and his impatience progressively develops into exasperation:

> **D** — You prefer the purer view that here at last is a painter who does not paint, does not pretend to paint. Come, come, my dear fellow, make some kind of connected statement and then go away.
>
> **B** — Would it not be enough if I simply went away?
>
> **D** — No. You have begun. Finish. Begin again and go on until you have finished. Then go away. Try and bear in mind that the subject is not yourself, nor the Sufist Al-Haqq, but a particular Dutchman by name van Velde, hitherto erroneously referred to as an artiste peintre.
>
> **B** — How would it be if I first said what I am pleased to fancy he is, fancy he does, and then that it is more than likely that he is and does quite otherwise? Would not that be an excellent issue out of all our afflictions? He happy, you happy, I happy, all three bubbling over with happiness.
>
> **D** — Do as you please. But get it over. (122–3)

Apart from explicit statements of disaffection or incredulity, the pressures that Beckett's theory exert on extant critical discourse is played out within the dialogues. Discourse is ruptured by the implications of this art of a different order, for given that it involves a plane "logically unavailable to the painter," there is presumably no means, or at least no adequate means, of discussing it. It is not simply the case that Duthuit loses patience with Beckett's anarchic posturings ("perhaps that is enough for today" (103)). Beckett, too, is apparently overwhelmed by the task he has set himself, and breaks down in a number of moments, the most notable being at the end of a strident rebuttal from Duthuit:

> **D** — Are we really to deplore the painting that is a rallying, among the things of time that pass and hurry us away, towards a time that endures and gives increase?
>
> **B** — (Exit weeping.) (113)

Beckett's affirmative response to the question "Are you suggesting that the painting of van Velde is inexpressive?" is recorded as being made "A fortnight later." (120) Rather like the situation of one of Beckett's own narrators, discourse (especially in the face of an art of the unintelligible) is forever in danger of breaking down:

B — For what is this coloured plane, that was not there before. I don't know what it is, having never seen anything like it before. It seems to have nothing to do with art, in any case, if my memories are correct. (Prepares to go)

D — Are you not forgetting something?

B — Surely that is enough?(126)

What is clearly at stake in the *Three Dialogues with Georges Duthuit* is something analogous with the very evasion of expression that underpins the theoretical project of both Bacon and Beckett. The continuity of discourse, the possibility of statement in the Beckett dialogues is characterized by a sense of imminent dysfunction. The dramatic enactment of the problems inherent in discussing a theory of art so aggressively at odds with the received assumptions of composition and criticism highlights the fundamental question of what relation criticism bears to art in the first place, and in this focuses the principal questions explored within postmodern theory: what exactly is critical discourse, and what is it expressive of?

Andrew Benjamin, in his revisionary study of mimesis, *Art, Mimesis and the Avant-Garde*, addresses this issue in terms of the examination of what an interpretive act is. Benjamin notes that interpretation cannot avoid being representational of representation, and as such is a repetitive act of similarity, rather than an originary act of difference:

> Such a conception of interpretation would have the inevitable consequence that the process (or practice) of interpretation would have thereby become that task whose object was to construct, either implicitly or explicitly, a homological relation between the object of interpretation and interpretation itself. One would still the other.[6]

Furthermore, Benjamin argues that the homological relationship between the object of interpretation and the act of interpretation is an important constitutive element of representation: the two are "interarticulated."[7] Beckett's and Bacon's respective theorizing of painting as an inexpressive, intransitive act implies that since there is no "object of interpretation" (how does one re(-)present in written form an intransitive, temporal act?) there can be no interarticulation. In terms of Benjamin's formulation of interpretation, the theory of painting as an inexpressive act signifies "the presence of an origin – a site – that resist(s) synthesis,"[8] an original "dis-unity" or becoming, beyond representation within the spatial domain of critical discourse. The Sylvester interviews bear out the obvious fact that the theory itself can be interarticulated, rendered homologous in the interpretive language of both Bacon and Sylvester.

The discursive aporias of the Duthuit dialogues, however, disclose the radical otherness of Beckett's theory, and its consequences for the interpretive act. Benjamin recognizes that the Sylvester interviews bring to the fore the problem of interpretation, but his interest is confined to the relationship between the discursive claims of the interviews and the paintings to which they refer. He does not address the possible consequences Bacon's theory might entail for critical discourse, though he acknowledges that his specific questions prefigure a much larger consideration. Both Bacon and Beckett propose a theory of art for which there is, literally, nothing to sustain interpretation as a viable act, constitutive or otherwise; or, another way of putting it, the spatiality of critical writing is at odds with pictorial time.

The Duthuit dialogues are expressive of the restless, heterogeneous stimulation of what Susan Sontag called the erotic, rather than hermeneutic engagement with art.[9] Sontag's prescriptive term, responsive to the "programmatic avant-gardism"[10] of the early 1960s, was suggested as a corrective to the transformative, but at the same time "never-consummated project of *interpretation*."[11] It is still highly appropriate in the current context, in that it invokes a stimulated process of engagement, a kinetic rather than static negotiation of that which constitutes the object of interpretation. Sontag asks the question, "What would criticism look like that would serve the work of art, not usurp its place?"[12] Poststructuralist moves such as the *autocritique* (Foucault's "The Order of Discourse"), the post-critical essay (Peter Gidal's *Understanding Beckett*) or the collage of samplings (Derrida's *Glas*), provide remarkable examples of critical practices that go a long way to reclaim the art work from being a "secondary effect" of interpretation.[13] The fact that poststructuralist strategies have been so contentious, and have been the object themselves of hostile interpretation, evidences the continued hegemony of traditional mimetic assumptions of interpretation.

Bacon's frustration at the impotence of criticism in relation to painting, (100) combined with his recognition that his theory is "far-out and impossible," (126) is the closest that he comes to facing the ferocious dilemma of expression. Beckett and Duthuit, though, are "skewered" on it. The point on which they writhe is that moment when the critical act can no longer keep abreast of the creative act, when criticism realizes that it cannot capture the dynamism of compulsion within its terminal frames of reference. Their dialogues evoke the absence of an "unbearable presence, unbearable because neither to be wooed nor to be stormed." (110–11)

1 Andrew Sinclair, *Francis Bacon. His Life and Violent Times* (London: Sinclair-Stevenson, 1993) p. 260.

2 Sinclair, p. 285.

3 Samuel Beckett, *Three Dialogues with Georges Duthuit* (London: John Calder, 1976) p. 109. Further references to this edition are given after quotations in the text.

4 David Sylvester, *The Brutality of Fact. Interviews with Francis Bacon* (London: Thames & Hudson, 1990) p. 89. Further references to this edition are given after quotations in the text.

5 Gilles Deleuze, *Francis Bacon: Logique de la Sensation* (Paris: Editions de la Difference, 1981.)

6 Andrew Benjamin, *Art, Mimesis and the Avant-Garde* (London: Routledge, 1991) p. 8.

7 ibid.

8 ibid.

9 Susan Sontag, "Against Interpretation," in *A Susan Sontag Reader* (Harmondsworth: Penguin, 1982) p. 104.

10 ibid., p. 101.

11 ibid., pp. 96–7.

12 ibid., p. 102.

13 Benjamin, p. 8.

[9] 'Unseizable Enigma': Notes Towards a New Morphology of the Image

I want to begin with a story about breasts. Most people are familiar with the films of Woody Allen, and the various on-screen personae that represent the director's trademark, angst-ridden hysteria. Allen's films represent a serial autobiography, depicting a very troubled individual whose psychopathology runs the gamut of disturbance, from neurosis to manic-depression and occasional bouts of psychosis. What is also well known is that before Allen's celebrated film career from the early 1970s onwards, he was an established stand-up comedian in New York City. Even at this early stage of his career as a celebrity Allen's psychological and emotional problems provided fodder for his comic routines. In one of his many sketches that deal with his childhood, he offers us, in a cathartic moment of self-revelation, an insight into why he is so messed up as an adult: he was "breast-fed from falsies."

Now as unassuming and irrelevant as this anecdote may at first seem, it provides us with a glimpse of a number of key concepts about photography that are challenged and even undermined by the new practices of digital reproduction and sampling, and the more dramatic techniques of digital photography and two and three dimensional rendering, both of which create photographic images without the intervention of the camera. Allen's childhood trauma, being breast-fed from falsies, raises all of the nihilistic issues that we readily associate with a certain tendency in postmodern culture: empty, depthless surfaces, floating signifiers, expenditure without return, the fake, or inauthentic copy, the disappearance of the real, the simulacrum, and so on. The idea that any form of cultural production in the name of postmodernism is a flaccid, counterfeit degradation of the values and principles of aesthetic making is very familiar, especially in the pronouncements of conservative art critics such as Hilton Kramer and Robert Hughes.

Digital image-making is a product of simulation technology and therefore falls within the gamut of this critique. More directly, the digital image is representative of a larger "crisis in perceptive faith" that has been precipitated by the rapid installation of electronic, telematic culture, where perception at a distance, or telesthesia, means that you don't have to be at the location of an event in order to experience a simulated perception of it.[1] This, in itself, is a symptom of the entire critique of presence that has preoccupied literary and cultural critics for the last thirty years. However, there is an alternative view of digital (re)productive technologies that regards new media as offering greater potential for the creation, capturing and dissemination of images and sees them as extending rather than obliterating the art of photography as we know it. If anything, the impact of digital technologies has heightened the long history of aesthetic debate surrounding photography as a visual medium by offering new insights into the nature not only of the photographic image, but, in the words of Paul Virilio, of all "regimes of the visual." (22)

The idea that digital technology *introduces*, or *initiates* a problematics of the photographic image is, of course, nonsense. Ever since Walter Benjamin's critique of the auratic glow of the artwork in the age of mechanical reproduction, the status of the photographic image as an objective, truthful depiction of a glimpse of reality has withered. So, too, has the notion of an original image that can claim authenticity over reproductions or fraudulent copies. In the age of mechanical and post-mechanical reproduction, the image is always already reproduced. This critique of photography as a metaphysics of presence can be traced back to the very origins of photography in the nineteenth century. The French sculptor Rodin argued that photography lies, since it holds time still. In this century, the critical writings of Roland Barthes, which amounted to a sustained, lifetime's attention to the conventionality of all signifying systems, fixed the idea that photography, like certain genres of painting, never corresponded to reality but rather generated a codified "reality effect." Photography's claims to veracity have been under attack for some time. The types of attack that have beset it are not peculiar to postmodernism, though they have typically been the principal interests of many practitioners of postmodern philosophy and cultural theory, especially in terms of the displacement of origins, and the bombardment of image-systems within the information economies of media-sophisticated, late twentieth-century culture. As Bill Mitchell, former director of MIT Media Lab, has suggested,

> Thus late in the century of Joyce and Borges, of cubism and surrealism, of Wittgenstein's loss of faith in logical positivism and of post-structuralism's gonzo metaphysics, the production of reproduction was again redefined. From the moment of its sesquicentennial in

1989 photography was dead—or, more precisely, radically and permanently displaced—as was painting 150 years before.[2]

Photography, of course, was said to be the death of painting. We should remember that the institutionalized teaching of fine art history within the twentieth century, certainly outside Europe at least, has been dependent upon photographed reproductions of original art works. As Robert Hughes indicates, the links between the tyranny of distance and questions of authenticity go hand in hand.[3] Those of us living in the antipodes, of course, have always had the reputation of being barbarians, and the spurious cultural legacy of a secondhand image-repertoire, as opposed to the gallery-tan from the aura of *qua* work of art, is a sign of our depleted cultural capital. Had we but world enough and time, things may well have been different.

The suggestion that both painting and photography are dead arts is based on a reconfiguration of the "successive phases of the image."[4] The critiques of the ontology of the image that emerged out of the nineteenth century, germinated in modernism and festered in postmodernism, are grounded in a fundamental premise of correspondence between image and referent, artifice and world; in other words, the classical, Platonic notion of the image as representation or likeness *of something*. Jean Baudrillard has summarized the successive phases of the image in the following way:

— it is the reflection of a basic reality
— it masks and perverts a basic reality
— it masks the *absence* of a basic reality
— it bears no relation to any reality whatever: it is its own pure simulacrum. (11)

The first two phases develop from the dominance of realism to styles such as Cubism in painting or photomontage and collage. The third indicates abstraction and the post-structuralist critique of presence (where the image *"plays at being* an appearance" (12)). The fourth "is no longer in the order of appearance at all" and registers the contemporary age of hyperrealism and simulation. (12)

It is in relation to simulation and the hyperreal phase of the image that digital photographic images, as I shall describe them, need to be understood. Before examining the various technologies of digital simulation, the images they produce and their significance for concepts such as originality, reproduction, authenticity, copyright and creativity, it is important to briefly sketch or review the concepts of hyperreality and the simulacrum.

The concept of simulation is, as I have already suggested, not an isolated or even new idea. It is implicit in our most ancient theories of the image, of appearance and representation. In the "Theory of Art" section of *The Republic*, Plato suggests that a painted image of a bed is three times removed from the reality it purports to represent. The actual bed of which it is a likeness is merely an attempted likeness of an ideal bed, or pure form, that exists in the world of being. He concludes that the "art of representation is therefore a long way removed from the truth, and is able to reproduce everything because it has little grasp of anything, and that little is of a mere phenomenal appearance."[5] In terms of Plato's theory of ideal forms, which exist in the higher, divine world of being, anything in the human world of becoming (what we might tentatively call reality) is defined from the outset in terms of reproduction. Implicit in Plato's account is the insight, in the inimitable words of Baudrillard, that "the real is not only what can be reproduced, but that which is always already reproduced." (146) In other words, in Plato's philosophy images are copies of things that don't have a basis in reality, they are "phantasms" or simulacra. The term simulacrum is, in fact, the most common translation of Plato's term phantasm, the copy of a copy. Baudrillard, of course, very rarely uses the term real (unless he is invoking the "desert of the real") and prefers the term hyperreal, which he defines as "models of a real without origin or reality." (2) While Baudrillard's prose can be notoriously turgid ("hyperrealism is the limit of art, and of the real, by respective exchange, on the level of the simulacrum") (147), he is actually working with fundamental concepts that we are familiar with from classical philosophy and aesthetics. In terms of the successive phases of the image already discussed, it is clear that they work on the principle of the binary opposition, the interplay of difference between two items, in which the identity of one is defined in terms of the other. The theory of appearance in classical philosophy is grounded in this idea, in that a representation that can be called a "good" likeness, a compelling, *trompe l'oeil* depiction of a thing, makes us forget that we are looking at a picture and convinces us that we are regarding a facet of the world, as if we are looking at it through a window. However, this assumes, first, that there is a unified reality that exists prior to its reproducibility, and secondly, that such a reality can be apprehended purely in a first-hand way. For cultural theorists such as Baudrillard and Umberto Eco, or media theorists such as Marshall McLuhan, our experience of the world is always mediated, such that the difference between the precession of media representation and actual world is, for all intents and purposes, non-existent. In this respect, the decisive difference between two elements, reality and appearance, has imploded. The hyperreal, then, is not so much a matter of recognizing that something is a copy of a real thing, but that the difference between copy and real thing no longer exists (some would argue no longer matters).

For example, when I was discussing this concept in class a number of years ago, a student of mine articulated his understanding of the hyperreal in terms of his experience of riding a motor-bike. He argued that you never, and can never, ride a motor-bike for the first time (even though he had only just purchased his machine and was, literally, riding it for the first time). He reflected, how do you ride it, like Steve McQueen, Peter Fonda, Marlon Brando, or Arnold Schwarzenegger? In other words, he felt totally self-conscious about getting on the thing and riding it, for it was as if he had already ridden it in the shadow of others, many times before, and didn't know how "he" should ride it. The theory of hyperreality would say that an ensemble of copies of the act of riding the bike, derived from popular culture, had preceded what, for the sake of argument, we can call the reality, since it no longer contains any decisive difference from the simulacra that precede it. There was for him no original, first-hand experience of riding a motorbike. Like Roland Barthes' famous description of myth as a language, the cultural experience of motorbike riding, which we may term the mopedular code, was itself a language system, a grammar of the *déjà parle*, the already said.

This instance of echolalia, or repeated statement, represents a much larger phenomenon within postmodern culture, the psychopathology of exhaustion, of depleted possibility. It stands for a situation in which any possible statement or instance of cultural production is already marked with the specter of its own self-consciousness as a quotation. Ours is an age of metalanguage, not language. Perhaps the most enduring account of this phenomenon, of the already said, is Umberto Eco's portrait of a "man who loves a very cultivated woman and knows he cannot say to her 'I love you madly,' because he knows that she knows (and that she knows that he knows) that these words have already been written by Barbara Cartland. Still, there is a solution. He can say, 'As Barbara Cartland would put it, I love you madly.'"[6]

With the hyperreal, then, we have what both Baudrillard and Virilio have called the "aesthetics of disappearance," the waning of reality in the face of disappearing distinctions between real thing and fake, original and copy (while the concept of the original is presumably something valuable, and its disappearance something to be mourned, there is at least one forger of old masters living in Venice who signs his forgeries as authentic fakes). The argument against much postmodern art, for example, is based on the principle of the artist as author, originator of a work that is brought into being through an act of making (in other words, the classical idea of the artist as poet or maker). It's not surprising that an artist such as Jeff Koons has become the whipping-boy of conservative art critics, for he not only promotes banality in his work, but also an unabashed disdain for the integrity of the creative act. Koons plays no role whatsoever in the physical act of artistic making, leaving such drudgery to artisans and craftsman. In claiming authorship of such work he is effectively making fraudulence an art form, though for his troubles he has generated little enthusiasm from mainstream art criticism. Anyone who saw *American Visions* will remember that for the entire duration of his interview with Koons, Robert Hughes kept the artiste of artlessness squirming on this very point. More than anything else, Hughes just wanted to get it straight for the record, from the porcelain horse's mouth, so to speak, that Koons plays absolutely no part in the process of *making* the work that bears his name.

There seems to be a bit more sympathy in the critical world for the image theft of Sherrie Levine, who infamously appropriates other people's photographs. Her work has irrefutably been taken seriously within literary and visual art criticism. It is typically characterized as offering an aggressive, impatient meta-critique of authorship, tradition and spectatorship. Her work has been described as "dramatizing the diminished possibilities for creativity in an image-saturated culture."[7] In putting her name to someone else's image, Levine specifically foregrounds the links, validated by copyright law, between creativity and paternity, the idea of the author as father or progenitor. In this respect her work is particularly relevant to the ethics and aesthetics of digital image making. In the words of the critic Gregory Ulmer, copyright to Levine "now means the right to copy anything."[8]

How, then, do these ideas relate to digital photography? Digital photography can be made in two ways. The first involves the taking of an image with a digital camera, which stores the image as binary data in a mini hard disk in the camera. This data is then uploaded directly into the CPU of a computer, which then displays it as pixels on a screen, which we then see as an image of the thing that was photographed. With digital photography there is no intermediate step of development nor is there of necessity a hard copy (new laser technologies do allow such images to be printed out, though it is arguable that the quality is as good as an image exposed directly on to film). The technological distinction between the traditional analogue photograph and the contemporary digital photograph is crucial here. A photograph that exposes light on to film is an analogue "representation of the differentiation of space in a scene" and "varies continuously, both spatially and tonally." As Mitchell explains, digital images are encoded by "uniformly subdividing the picture plane into a finite Cartesian grid of cells (known as *pixels*) and specifying the intensity of color of each cell by means of an integer number drawn from some limited range." (4-5) In this respect, the digital photograph, like all digital information, occupies a purely abstract state, only temporarily manifesting itself as a visible image, but for the most part remaining stored in a latent state as infravisible data. While this flickering of presence and absence, marking and erasure, may at first seem to disqualify it as a photograph (which we typically hold in our hand as a fixed object of perception), we should remember that the writing of light on a receptive surface (photo-*graphy*) is the procedure that unites both analogue and digital photography. All that has changed is the type of writing surface, as well as a shift in the culture of apprehension (how we engage with and view photographic images) from permanence to ephemerality.

The second type of digital photograph is more dramatic and, as I've already suggested, needs to be considered in the light of the previous discussion of hyperreality. It involves a series of simulation procedures, conducted entirely within the computer, which create, in Virilio's words, "*synthetic images*, products of info-graphic software." (62) The computer enables the creation of what Mitchell has called "photograph-like digital images," or "fake photographs," (19) depending on your point of view and degree of sympathy for the ethics and aesthetics of virtual technologies. It is in relation to the latter, of course, that most of the problems concerning technologies of simulation arise. It is impossible to tell any difference between a printed image in a newspaper and its digital equivalent. Digital *aficionados* celebrate this flawless mimicry in exultant tones, taking a perverse pleasure in the artificial and the counterfeit, as if it is in some way natural.

In his remarkable book *The Reconfigured Eye*, Bill Mitchell examines the implications of what he calls "visual truth in the post-photographic era." Sophisticated graphic and simulation software enable anyone skilled in their use to create a complete virtual, photographic studio entirely within the confines of their computer. Working with a computer-generated, three dimensional model, for example, is to work in a virtual world:

> We can make images of the contents of this world by introducing a virtual camera and virtual lights, then computing a synthetic photograph. To the extent that the geometric model and its virtual lighting are sufficiently accurate, the synthetic photograph will resemble a real one. (124)

Although 2D and 3D rendering make effective use of externally produced images that have been scanned into the computer, they are not dependent upon it. The post-photographic era is the time of the cameraless photograph.

The idea of the cameraless photograph explicitly demonstrates Virilio's notion of a crisis in perceptive faith, for it offers "sightless vision," "optical imagery with no apparent base." (59) It is the ultimate perfect copy of an absent reality. The "automation of perception" (59) is something Virilio has written about in numerous books, and it is related to the development of telecommunications culture, a process of remote sensing and accelerated perception that goes back to the invention of the telescope. (4) In terms of photography specifically, the implications of this "artificial vision" are profound and, potentially, disturbing. (59) The simulated photograph represents, in Virilio's terms, a "solemn farewell to the man behind the camera, the complete evaporation of visual subjectivity into ambient technical effect." (47) Mitchell offers a similar observation, arguing that with a digital image the "distinction between the causal process of the camera and the intentional process of the artist can no longer be drawn so confidently and categorically." (31) Many of the problems associated with digital photography can be overcome by simply regarding the process of electronic simulation as an enabling technology, an apparatus that allows someone to make an image, just as an ordinary camera does. The end result, as with analogue photography, is a picture on the wall (or on the screen), the culmination of a series of technological processes.

However a digital photograph is not something that is *taken*, in the way that we take an analogue photograph. To take a photograph is to capture a memory of light. The digital image doesn't capture light but programs it. It is very much a synthetic image, something made, assembled, grafted. If, as Baudrillard suggests, the analogue photograph "retains the moment of disappearance," then in the synthetic image "the real has already disappeared."[9] The processes available for the fabrication of synthetic or electronic photographs involve the manipulation of existing images or objects that have been scanned into the computer or the simulation of images and objects using two and/or three dimensional rendering software. Both practices invariably call to mind strategies of appropriation, sampling and recombination that have become the signature of much art of the last two decades, at least. It is this readymade aesthetic that prompted Mitchell to suggest that digital image-making is typically postmodern, since it "privileges fragmentation, indeterminacy, and heterogeneity, and ... emphasizes process or performance rather than the finished art object." (8)

With digitization, recombinant processes such as sampling and collage enter into an entirely new realm of possibility. By its very nature binary data is highly susceptible to change, manipulation and reconstitution. It's so easy to touch up, correct, alter, distort, falsify, tamper with and improve digital images, as well as deftly conceal all the seams and signs of manipulation. Digital deception has become an art form in itself, particularly in the world of advertising, as evidenced in the infamous digital treatments of celebrities and world leaders by the Benetton Corporation. The degree of self-conscious image-play within the "United Colors of Benetton" campaign has led to the creation of virtual, anti-advertising. As the Australian writer Paula Amad has suggested, the actual products that Benetton are purporting to sell have little or no presence within any given ad. Consequently, as advertisements they "can't get around the problem of representation's relation to the real."[10]

Sophisticated techniques of image-enhancement have become part of the arsenal of image hackers and culture jammers determined to use media to combat the rhetorical, corporate power of the media-scape we live in. In a variation on Gerald Graff's theme of "literature against itself," countercultural practices such as "billboard banditry," which often exploit image manipulation, are instances of media being used against itself, as critics such as Douglas Rushkoff and Mark Dery[11] have shown. On the down side, such feats of trickery and illusion, whether in the press or fringe-culture, merely reinforce the argument that digital imagery is a low form of fakery, of deceit, that can mislead and ultimately have deleterious effects.

Appropriation, sampling and Situationist-style collage, though, have powerful aesthetic potential for artists working in the field of digital image-making. The New Zealand-born artist Murray McKeich approaches digital technology first and foremost as an artist, whose medium, at this point in time, happens to be computer graphics. McKeich's work is characterized by a strong, recombinant aesthetic, the mixing and mingling of strange and discordant elements, of unlikely objects in incongruous contexts. His talisman is that wonderful line from the proto-Surrealist writer Isidore Ducasse, the Comte de Lautréamont, who wrote in his *Songs of Maldoror* of "the chance encounter, on an operating table, of a sewing machine and an umbrella." McKeich's imagination is well *served* by the specialized techniques of morphing, combination, and displacement mapping that software such as *Photoshop* enable, as well as the ability to generate three-dimensional images of his own invention, using 3-D rendering software. However no software can replace genuine creative force. This is amply evidenced by many of the pedestrian attempts at digital image-making around, that invariably betray their genesis in *Photoshop* or *Illustrator*. With McKeich we only see the eloquence of skilled rendering, *trompe l'oeil* spectacles that fool the eye as well as engage it with energized strangeness.

In McKeich's work we find all the techniques of what Mitchell refers to as "electro-bricolage," where the detritus of industrial process is blended with historical animal portraiture to produce a cybernetic vision of the apocalypse. Similarly, image and texture mapping, relief textures, smooth shading and directional highlighting combine to create brilliant three dimensional assemblages that, while unlike anything we have seen, look compellingly real. They look, in fact, as if they could be real. His images

MURRAY McKEICH, Untitled (detail). Courtesy the artist.

simulate how such realities would look if photographed.

Such images testify to the "paradoxical presence" of the digital image theorized by Virilio, (63) the "unseizable enigma" that gives this essay its title.[12] The image is very much there, visible to the eye as a captured object, caught at the very moment of its passing, as in the taking of a photograph. But at the same time it isn't there at all. Its photo-similitude is the result of a complex variation of differential intensities of light and shade within the grid of screen pixels. If we blow the image up, *à la* Antonioni, we find that we get less information than we actually had before, and it doesn't reveal hidden secrets, for the vivid detail starts to break down to gradations of tone within a highly regimented grid made up of square picture elements.

McKeich's images are irresistibly synthetic. However, they are different from the synthetic imagery of artists Troy Innocent, Linda Dement or Jon McCormack, which makes no attempt to in any way look photorealistic. McKeich's work is hyperreal in the sense that I have been discussing the term. It brings to enigmatic presence virtual photos of vivid realities that have no basis in reality. In this respect, the term hyperreal loses some of its negative capital, and starts to acquire a more appealing connotation of skilled artifice. In the words of Paul Virilio

To my mind, this is one of the most crucial aspects of the development of the new technologies of digital imagery and of the synthetic vision offered by electron optics: the relative fusion/confusion of the factual ... and the virtual; the ascendancy of the 'reality effect' over a reality principle already largely contested elsewhere, particularly in physics. (60)

I have been focussing on the work of Virilio and Mitchell throughout this discussion because they have both, in their own ways, offered incisive critiques of the implications of digitization for the technology and practice of photography. But they have also initiated a broader discussion of a new morphology of perception that is somehow peculiar to the age of information networks, remote sensing, and the boundary metaphysics brought about by the advent of cybernetics. The post-photographic age is also the post-human age, and if the rhetoric of the Canadian political scientist Arthur Kroker is to believed, just about everyone wants to be a cybernetic organism, complete with Stelarcian third-hand and bodily prosthetics to die for. Reading too-cool-for-their-own-good cyber-dudes such as Kroker, or virtual virtuosi such as Nicholas Negroponte, you would be forgiven for thinking that the technological future they desiderate is assured, and that once achieved, it will be business as usual for humans, in their technologically augmented forms. What they fail to realize, however, is that disciplines such as cybernetics offer uncertainty, indeterminacy and confusion of philosophical categories, not alternative certainties in the name of cyberspace.

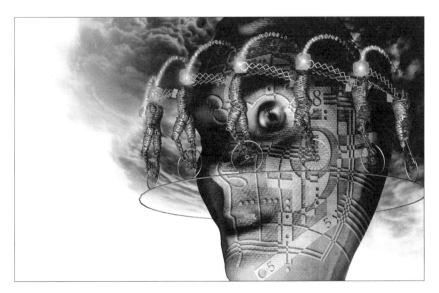

MURRAY McKEICH, Untitled. Courtesy the artist

95

The ambivalent blurring of the hyperreal is very much in evidence in cyberculture. While its rhetoricians are busy likening people to machines, and transforming machines into artificially intelligent beings, cyberculture persistently skirts margins and peripheries rather than achieves stable centers. No one understood this better than the science fiction writer Philip K. Dick, whose prolific and varied output can be read as a prescient allegory of the emergent cybercultural world that seems to be forming around us. Dick wrote heaps of stories about androids, cyborgs and other synthetic constructs that confuse with their appearance and masquerade as people. The general term that he used to describe these chimaera was "simulacra." Surprise surprise.

When identity, essence and psychopathology are aligned with appearance, with the seemliness of things, metaphysical certainties, binary oppositions and reassurance go out the window. It's a bit like René Magritte's *La Clef des Champs*, the referent no longer adheres to the image, leaving floating, or splintered signifiers that have no anchoring in reliable, normative systems of understanding. This is the real ambience of cyberculture, the unknowable. If you want to push the Douglas Rushkoff line, you could say that cyberculture is a cultural virus, a meme, a virulent strain of metaphysical contagion that threatens to infiltrate the body politic and break down the reliable certainties that we live by. If you don't want to go that far, to "pathologize the media,"[13] then you can say that it's like digital photography, a form of synthetic experience that turns reality and traditional forms of representation on their head. Virilio argues that "we still cannot seem to get a grip on the *virtualities* of the paradoxical logic of the videogram, the hologram or digital imagery." (63) No matter how far we can reclaim the digital photograph, which we should perhaps rename the photogram, it is still a highly problematic and contentious phenomenon. In this it is a metonymy of the cybercultural age, a signification of *apparent* reality. Apparent reality is more difficult to distinguish from actuality, since it is readily accepted as being reality. It is much more seemly than a virtual world. Apparent reality, like hyperreality, is more insidious, convincing people that the inauthentic and the fake are genuine, that the authentic and the original are fake. How can we be sure that the *Mona Lisa* we see in the Louvre is not a copy? The fact that we can't be sure reveals something of the beguiling machinations of apparent reality. Apparent reality endures well. The same is true of any photograph that you may see from now on. You just never know. With the ambiguous presence of the hyperreal all around us, the best you can hope for is that it *might* be real.

Which brings us back to breasts. Greg Ulmer has referred to the giving and taking away of the breast in childhood as the first digital act.[14] Reminiscent of Freud's famous *fort/da* narrative of possession and loss, this moment of abjection, of having and losing, presence and absence, is in effect the essence of digitality. The binary logic that drives the computerized, electronic world, is based on Boolean algebra, the symbolic logic invented by the nineteenth century British mathematician George Boole. Boolean algebra works on a strict binary opposition that equates a digit with a value of electric signal being either present or absent: 1 is present, 0 absent. It's hardly surprising that Woody Allen's characters are so confused. At least one prominent example of postmodern art comes to mind in this context. Cindy Sherman's representation of breasts and breast-feeding in some of her historical portraits are highly suggestive of this interplay of presence and absence. Sherman's mothers and daughters are united by an ambiguous and tentative bond, in which the breast is merely a sign, the mark of an absent presence.

CINDY SHERMAN, Untitled # 216, 1989. Courtesy the artist and Metro Pictures, New York.

The digital image, or photogram, is caught in the midst of this oscillation between presence and absence. It is a form of vision without sight, perception ungrounded in experience. A synthetic, apparent reality without depth. In *Camera Lucida*, Barthes argues that photography, unlike painting, requires the presence of a real thing, something "that-has-been." Almost two decades after Barthes wrote this, we can say that digital photography, like painting, can now "feign reality without having seen it." In the digital world, we can say that the name of photography's *noeme* is "that-has-never-been."[15]

The dilemma for theoreticians of photography is that digital images still involve writing with light. In terms of Barthes' notion of the adherence of the image, the digital photogram is in no way different, for both are enigmas, unseizable, paradoxical presences. In both, a referent adheres and is indistinguishable from the image itself. As Barthes describes this effect,

> It is as if the Photograph always carries its referent with itself, both affected by the same amorous or funereal immobility, at the very heart of the moving world: they are glued together, limb by limb, like the condemned man and the corpse in certain tortures ... The Photograph belongs to that class of laminated objects whose two leaves cannot be separated without destroying them both: the windowpane and the landscape. (5–6)

No matter how simulated or artificial photo-visual imagery is, it cannot escape the "stubbornness of the Referent in always being there." (6)

Bill Mitchell advances that "as we enter the post-photographic era, we must face once again the ineradicable fragility of our ontological distinctions between the imaginary and the real." (225) At the conclusion of *The Reconfigured Eye*, we end up, not surprisingly, back in Plato's cave, where this whole mess started. "We have indeed learned to fix shadows, but not to secure their meanings or to stabilize their truth values." (225) So here we are again, watching shadows on the wall.

1 Paul Virilio, *The Vision Machine* (London: British Film Institute, 1994) p. 75. Further references to this edition are given after quotations in the text.

2 Bill Mitchell, *The Reconfigured Eye. Visual Truth in the Post-Photographic Era* (Cambridge, Mass.: MIT Press, 1994) p. 20. Further references to this edition are given after quotations in the text.

3 Robert Hughes, *Nothing If Not Critical. Essays on Art and Artists* (London: Collins Harvill, 1990) p. 4.

4 Jean Baudrillard, *Simulations*, trans. P. Foss, P. Patton & P. Beitchman (New York: Semiotext(e), 1993) p. 11. Further references to this edition are given after quotations in the text.

5 Plato, *The Republic*, trans. D. Lee (Harmondsworth: Penguin, 1987) p. 426.

6 Umberto Eco, *Reflections on the Name of the Rose* (London: Secker & Warburg, 1985) p. 67.

7 Craig Owens, "The Discourse of Others: Feminists and Postmodernism," in Hal Foster, ed. *The Anti-Aesthetic. Essays on Postmodern Culture* (Seattle: Bay Press, 1989) p. 73.

8 Gregory Ulmer, "The Object of Post-Criticism," in Foster, p. 96.

9 Jean Baudrillard, "The Art of Disappearance," trans. N. Zurbrugg, *World Art*, November (1994) p. 81.

10 Paula Amad, "'Where On Earth Would You Like To Be?' Explorations of Virtuality in Benetton Advertising," paper presented at the *Virtual Cultures* conference (convened by McKenzie Wark) Artspace, Sydney, 13 July (1996) p. 2.

11 See Douglas Rushkoff, *Media Virus. Hidden Agendas in Popular Culture* (Milsons Point, Random House, 1994) and Mark Dery, "Culture Jamming: Hacking, Slashing and Sniping in the Empire of Signs," *Open Magazine* Pamphlet Series, #25 (Westfield: New Jersey, 1993).

12 Baudrillard, 1994, p. 81.

13 McKenzie Wark, quoted in Phillip Adams, "Virtual Geography," interview with McKenzie Wark and Darren Tofts, *21C*, 1 (1996) p. 35.

14 Gregory Ulmer, "Florida Tablature: From Homepage to Barscreen," paper presented at the Power Institute of Fine Arts, Sydney University, 15 August (1995).

15 Roland Barthes, *Camera Lucida. Reflections on Photography*, trans. R. Howard (London: Fontana, 1982) p. 76. Further references to this edition are given after quotations in the text.

[10] The Passion of Andres Serrano

On October 11, 1997, a Sydney man walked into the National Gallery of Victoria. Without arousing the suspicion of attendants, he removed a photograph from the gallery wall and proceeded to stomp it into oblivion. The work in question was Andres Serrano's *Piss Christ*, one of a number of the artist's works included in the retrospective exhibition *A History of Serrano*. Twenty-four hours after this incident *Piss Christ* was the subject of another attack, only this time a hammer rather than a foot was applied. The shattered work was taken from the gallery and the exhibition was closed by gallery director Dr Timothy Potts, barely three days after it had opened. These events occurred amid highly publicized attempts by Catholic Church leaders and their supporters to prevent the work from being shown. The whole thing had rapidly become a media event, and Andres Serrano was once again at the center of a controversy.

So much has been written on the Serrano affair that it is virtually impossible to discuss it without feeling the oppressive weight of the anxiety of influence. The debate has cast its shadow wide, and any assertion runs the risk of being already said. I became acutely conscious of this when I typed out a possible opening gambit, after Foucault, after Magritte (here we go), "This is not a crucifix." This move, while predictable, was doubly useful in that it drew on contemporary theories concerning images, reality, reference, authenticity and originality, and at the same time contextualized debate by invoking a theme *de rigueur* in public discourse, that of sophistry (don't worry, it's not a real crucifix, just an image of one). It allowed me, in other words, to comment on the debate, and relieved me of the arduous duty of attempting to add something new to it. However, in an epiphany worthy of Marge Simpson, I quickly realized that my stratagem was simply replaying, with a twist, Robert Hughes' "*ceci n'est pas un Dieu*" from his 1993 book *Culture of Complaint*, which was in itself a printed version of a lecture given by Hughes at the New York Public Library in January 1992.

This vertigo of repetition soon became more of a focal issue for the Serrano affair than I had first thought.

To anyone familiar with the history of the reception of *Piss Christ* in the United States in the late 1980s, it is clear that its Melbourne reception was less an event than a re-run, what Serrano himself described as an "old hat" media event replaying a sense of moral and religious indignation that occurred elsewhere. Serrano's weariness in response to the whole thing was hardly surprising. There was something very tawdry about the unfolding of this re-hash of an outdated American drama, with George Pell playing understudy to the Rev. Donald Wildmon, and the Australian Family Association standing in as body-politic double for its American counterpart. Re-run ennui was also apparent in the religious bigotry of the two fanatics *manqués* who brought the whole thing to a head. Their misguided lipservice to patriotic moral outrage ("This guy can't be allowed to do this in my country") lacked conviction in the light of their appearance as voguish homeboys, not to mention their promotion of Melbourne as a Southern backwater, a hicktown of redneck crackers, convinced that public display of a picture of a Ku Klux Klansman would lead to racism.

There were some differences that made the Melbourne event distinctive. It was the first time *Piss Christ* has ever been physically attacked, and also the first time a Serrano show had been cancelled anywhere in the world. That should really put Melbourne on the map. Regardless of what one thinks of Serrano as an artist, the media event that emerged around *Piss Christ* portrayed Serrano as a one-hit wonder, and *A History of Serrano* as a one work retrospective. Apart from sensation-seeking overtures to licentiousness and perversity, the *History of Sex* exhibition at the Kirkcaldy Davies Gallery was hardly mentioned. Similarly, the National Gallery of Victoria was taken to task by critics of the situation for not sufficiently preparing its staff and the public for the potential offensiveness of Serrano's work (staff were purportedly given a day's notice on the protocols of complaint management). In failing to provide the kind of preparation that went into the Museum of Contemporary Art's Robert Mapplethorpe exhibition of 1995, the National Gallery of Victoria seemed to be assuming that the Melbourne art-going public was a homogenous wild bunch, aficionados of affrontery turned on to cutting edge treatments of the pornosophical image. These dubious distinctions are, in fact, the most troubling and demoralizing features of the whole Serrano fracas with the National Gallery of Victoria. It is with tremendous regret that we must concede that Melbourne is not New York or Sydney, and does have an unfortunate history of regressive art conservatism, to which we can now add the Second Coming of Andres Serrano.

Andres Serrano with *Piss Christ*, photograph by Sebastian Costanzo, 1997. Courtesy *The Age*.

Having said that, though, it must be conceded that any artist working with heavily charged icons, such as the crucifixion, will always be open to public censure. No matter how tiresome Serrano found the whole controversy in Melbourne, his incredulity is a little out of place, especially when his work is exhibited in a country for the first time. But this is not to make any concessions to censorship or the devaluation of art. I'd like to think that Melbourne is a sophisticated, intellectually robust city capable of intelligent, considered engagement with tough social, cultural, political and religious issues, especially as they are dramatized through art forms, such as photography. I am not in the least bit perturbed by interpretations of *Piss Christ* which emphasised its iconoclasm. My own childhood experience of the Catholic world view has led me to regard controversial treatments of Catholic iconography as legitimate and necessary critiques of an insidious, demeaning and repressive regime, which, in the final analysis, is a retreat from the world of lived experience. As a powerful text that defamiliarizes an image saturated with the weight of history, and therefore impunity, *Piss Christ*'s impact is unquestioned; the title alone is a guarantee of that. Catholicism is an act of forgetting as much as anything else, and Serrano's images constitute, among other things, wilful prompts to remembrance. There is more gore in Sam Peckinpah or Quentin Tarantino than in the contemporary trade in crucifixion iconography. Serrano is surely right in identifying the crucifixion with the expulsion of bodily fluids, as in medieval representations of the Passion, which often featured the body of Christ as a jellied mass covered in blood and the urine of Roman centurions. This is not to say, of course, that this is all there is to the image. *Piss Christ*'s value as art, as an aesthetic object, and the possible readings that can be made of it, are necessarily relative and contingent. It may well stand for the degeneration of modern art, as Robert Hughes has suggested in *American Visions*, the rictus at the end of a century of art that has lost track of its mission. It may also be a sublime testament to Christian sacrifice, were it not for the title. However, its relevance as a commentary on, and critique of, a particular belief system is very powerful and deeply personal to many who have regarded it and reflected upon it.

The Serrano debacle has certainly announced to the world that Melbourne has difficulty coping with such art, especially with art that forces people to think beyond dogma and narrow-mindedness, and challenges taken for granted assumptions through provocative, disturbing images. This is a function that modern art has always fulfilled, and should continue to fulfil, especially as new modes of thought, alternative ways of living, and different forms of sensibility are being defined and negotiated. Debates, then, to do with censorship, pornography, blasphemy and freedom of speech, have been done to death in discussions of Serrano. It is actually more instructive to see the harrying of *Piss Christ*, and the harrowing of Serrano, as a remake of the Passion of Christ. Public humiliation and the persecution of those who hold unpopular views are central to the Catholicism which produced Serrano and are also played out in *Piss Christ* and its contexts of reception. Serrano espouses a typically modern conception of the artist as one called to a vocation, as a priest to the order. In casting himself as a religious artist whose work is deeply misunderstood and misinterpreted, Serrano invokes the historical portrait of Christ as a controversial agitator, whose teachings and world-view were also misunderstood in his own time. *Piss Christ* was not damaged, it was desecrated.

In this postmodern mystery play, proceedings began in ritual fashion by declaring the essential Catholic belief in transubstantiation, the symbolic embodiment of the deity in the host of a worldly object. *Piss Christ* was the substantial manifestation of Serrano's values and ideas, and as such acquired an unholy, anti-sacramental significance. Its turbulent and intensive passage along the Via Dolorosa of media scrutiny and public debate enacted a dramatic parable concerning difference and unpopular opinion. When that 16-year-old zealot tolchocked *Piss Christ* it was not a moral but a eucharistic act, a stage in the assault and battery of the body of Christ (ranters failed to notice the potential heresy of stamping on and then taking a hammer to Catholicism's focal icon). When this innocent, who was not of admissible age, entered the gallery packing heat, the writing for Serrano and his Passion was already on the wall: "suffer the little children to come unto me."

The desecration of *Piss Christ* was not the culmination of the Passion, but an intermediate event, the seventh station of the cross, in which Christ falls for the second time. Serrano's travail along the road to Calvary is quite clear in the scriptural narrative I gleaned from the biblia of news print:

1st station: Catholic Archbishop of Melbourne Dr George Pell washes his hands of Serrano and condemns him.

2nd station: In a three-hour Supreme Court hearing, Serrano receives a cross to bear, the stain of common law misdemeanor and blasphemous libel.

3rd station: Serrano falls for the first time and is trampled on by John Allen Haywood.

4th station: Serrano is given matriarchal solace by one of his supporters: "the controversial photographs of religious icons immersed in bodily fluids seemed to me quite beautiful as works of art."

5th station: National Gallery of Victoria director Dr Timothy Potts defends Serrano and eases his burden by re-hanging the fallen *Piss Christ*.

6th station: Serrano wipes his brow in a gesture of relief, "Whew!"

7th station: Serrano falls for the second time. *Piss Christ* is taken down and leans in a corner of the gallery after being attacked with a hammer.

8th station: *A History of Serrano* is cancelled. Serrano exhorts the people of Melbourne to make a "great sacrifice" in his name and boycott the National Gallery's Rembrandt exhibition.

9th station: Betrayed by the trustees of the NGV, Serrano falls for the third time.

10th station: Denuded, Serrano bares his ignominy to a divided public.

11th station: Serrano is nailed to a wall before witnesses. At the ninth hour, he averts his eyes to heaven and beseeches, "Oh Lord, please don't let me be misunderstood."

12th station: Mute and impassive, Serrano is frozen in a barrage of press photographs, which fix him for eternity as a martyr to artistic integrity.

13th station: In a solemn pieta, Serrano's body is presented to conservators for inspection and assessment.

14th station: Serrano is buried in a "spineless" display of compromise and cultural terrorism.

Appearing to his followers after harrowing his own private hell, Serrano announces plans for a new Jerusalem, in which the battered *Piss Christ* will feature as a homage, unwitting or otherwise, to one of his heroes, the patron saint of smashed glass, Marcel Duchamp. A fitting act of appropriation when you think about it. To those of us left behind, what's left? Perhaps an Elvis-like resurrection cult? Or a tradition of folk ballads in the mode of "I dreamed I saw Andres Serrano last night." Maybe, too, the National Gallery of Victoria should now be thought of as a sacred site, of sorts, and be appropriately renamed Golgotha.

Index